LSAT®

PrepTest 85

Unlocked

Deconstructing the September 2018 LSAT

© 2019 by Kaplan, Inc.

Published by Kaplan Publishing, a division of Kaplan, Inc.
750 Third Avenue
New York, NY 10017

ISBN: 978-1-5062-4717-5
10 9 8 7 6 5 4 3 2 1

Table of Contents

The Inside Story 1

Section I: Reading Comprehension. 7

Section II: Logical Reasoning 25

Section III: Logical Reasoning. 39

Section IV: Logic Games 51

Glossary 63

The Inside Story

PrepTest 85 was administered in September 2018. What made this test so hard? Here's a breakdown of what Kaplan students who were surveyed after taking the official exam considered PrepTest 85's most difficult section.

Hardest PrepTest 85 Section as Reported by Test Takers

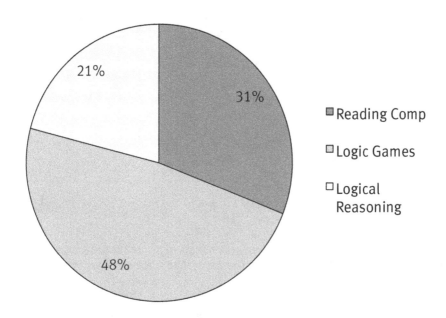

Based on these results, you might think that studying Logic Games is the key to LSAT success. Well, Logic Games is important, but test takers' perceptions don't tell the whole story. For that, you need to consider students' actual performance. The following chart shows the average number of students to miss each question in each of PrepTest 85's different sections.

Percentage Incorrect by PrepTest 85 Section Type

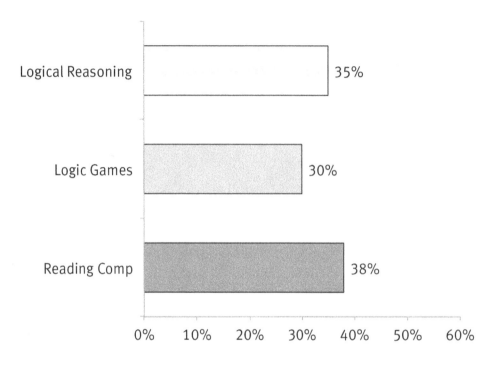

Actual student performance tells quite a different story. On average, students were more likely to miss questions in both Logical Reasoning and Reading Comprehension than they were in Logic Games, despite student perception that Logic Games was significantly more difficult.

Maybe students overestimate the difficulty of the Logic Games section because it's so unusual, or maybe it's because a really hard Logic Game is so easy to remember after the test. The truth is that the testmaker places hard questions throughout the test. Here were the locations of the 10 hardest (most missed) questions in the exam.

Location of the 10 Most Difficult Questions in PrepTest 85

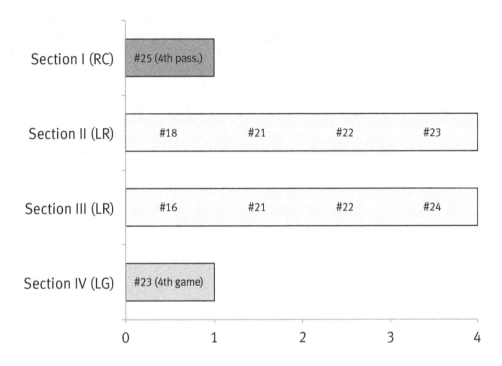

The takeaway from this data is that, to maximize your potential on the LSAT, you need to take a comprehensive approach. Test yourself rigorously, and review your performance on every section of the test. Kaplan's LSAT explanations provide the expertise and insight you need to fully understand your results. The explanations are written and edited by a team of LSAT experts, who have helped thousands of students improve their scores. Kaplan always provides data-driven analysis of the test, ranking the difficulty of every question based on actual student performance. The 10 hardest questions on every test are highlighted with a 4-star difficulty rating, the highest we give. The analysis breaks down the remaining questions into 1-, 2-, and 3-star ratings so that you can compare your performance to thousands of other test takers on all LSAC material.

Don't settle for wondering whether a question was really as hard as it seemed to you. Analyze the test with real data, and learn the secrets and strategies that help top scorers master the LSAT.

7 Can't-Miss Features of PrepTest 85

- With 11 Strengthen/Weaken questions, PT 85 was only the second test of the last 10 years with that many on a single LSAT. The other time was in December 2014 (PT 74).
- Those 11 Strengthen/Weaken questions, combined with 9 Flaw questions and 7 Assumption questions, yielded a total of 27 Assumption Family questions. That ties the high mark of the last 10 years. October 2011 (PT 64) and June 2015 (PT 75) also had 27.
- After a total of 13 Point at Issue questions on the three previous released tests, PT 85 only had 1 of them.
- PT 85 featured two Distribution games for only the sixth time ever.
- It was also the second test ever to pair its two Distribution games with two Strict Sequencing games. The other one was in June 1996 (PT 19).
- Prior to PT 85, there had only ever been two Evaluate the Argument questions in the Reading Comprehension section (one on PT 70 and one on PT 78). PT 85 doubled that number, containing two of them.
- Question 26 in Section II is about an auto insurance company with a multitude of commercial campaigns. For a study break, check out the likely inspiration for the stimulus: There's a Wikipedia page on GEICO advertising campaigns.

PrepTest 85 in Context

As much fun as it is to find out what makes a PrepTest unique or noteworthy, it's even more important to know just how representative it is of other LSAT administrations (and, thus, how likely it is to be representative of the exam you will face on Test Day). The following charts compare the numbers of each kind of question and game on PrepTest 85 to the average numbers seen on all officially released LSATs administered over the past five years (from 2013 through 2017).

Number of LR Questions by Type: PrepTest 85 vs. 2013–2017 Average

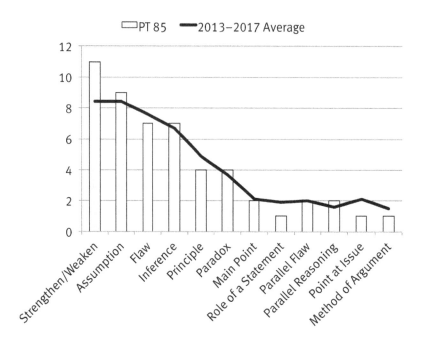

KAPLAN

Number of LG Games by Type: PrepTest 85 vs. 2013–2017 Average

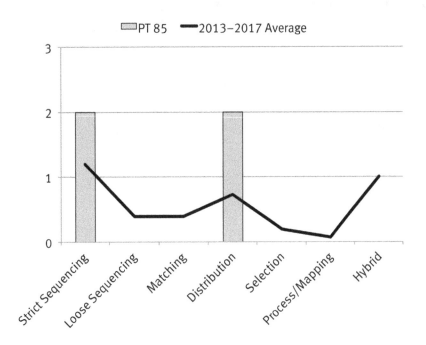

Number of RC Questions by Type: PrepTest 85 vs. 2013–2017 Average

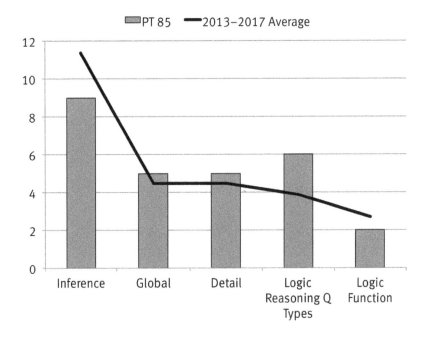

There isn't usually a huge difference in the distribution of questions from LSAT to LSAT, but if this test seems harder (or easier) to you than another you've taken, compare the number of questions of the types on which you, personally, are strongest and weakest. Then, explore within each section to see if your best or worst question types came earlier or later.

Students in Kaplan's comprehensive LSAT courses have access to every released LSAT and to a library of thousands of officially released questions arranged by question, game, and passage type. If you are studying on your own, you have to do a bit more work to identify your strengths and your areas of opportunity. Quantitative analysis (like that in the charts shown here) is an important tool for understanding how the test is constructed, and how you are performing on it.

Section I: Reading Comprehension

Passage 1: The Problem with *Shelley v. Kraemer*

Q#	Question Type	Correct	Difficulty
1	Global	A	★
2	Logic Reasoning (Evaluate the Argument)	B	★★
3	Inference	E	★
4	Logic Reasoning (Parallel Reasoning)	C	★★★
5	Logic Function	B	★★★
6	Logic Reasoning (Principle)	D	★★★

Passage 2: Did the Botai Ride Horses?

Q#	Question Type	Correct	Difficulty
7	Global	C	★
8	Inference	B	★★
9	Inference	E	★
10	Inference	C	★★★
11	Inference	D	★
12	Logic Function	A	★
13	Global	D	★★
14	Logic Reasoning (Evaluate the Argument)	A	★★

Passage 3: The Effect of Combining Music and Words

Q#	Question Type	Correct	Difficulty
15	Global	D	★★
16	Detail	C	★
17	Detail	E	★
18	Inference	D	★★
19	Logic Reasoning (Principle)	A	★★★
20	Detail	E	★★
21	Inference	B	★★★

Passage 4: Subduction and Earthquake Frequency

Q#	Question Type	Correct	Difficulty
22	Global	B	★★★
23	Detail	D	★★
24	Logic Reasoning (Weaken)	C	★★★
25	Inference	E	★★★★
26	Detail	C	★★★
27	Inference	E	★★★

Passage 1: The Problem with *Shelley v. Kraemer*

Step 1: Read the Passage Strategically
Sample Roadmap

line #	Keyword/phrase	¶ Margin notes
2	famously disallowed	S.v.K. - covenants can't discriminate
7	Because	
9	justly celebrated; overturning; key	
10	However	Au: ruling good but problem w/rationale
13	nevertheless; problematic	
15		Based on 14th Amendment
17	long been held	
18	but not	
19	But	But, state action?
22	?; although	
24	violated	Court: state enforces, and enforcement is unconstitutional
25	Because	
26	should	
27	According to	
30	Because	
32	followed	
35	threatened	
39	After all	Au: logic blurs private vs. state
44	Primarily, for this reason	Courts no longer use this logic
48	For instance	
54	Additionally; particularly noxious	Au: another problem
55	namely	
56	conclusion	
58	thus failed to target	
59	genuine problem	Court ignored the real issue of discrimination
60	troubling; not	
61	not	

KAPLAN

Discussion

This passage immediately introduces the **Topic**: the Supreme Court ruling in *Shelley v. Kraemer*. The ruling prevented states from enforcing covenants, deed restrictions that use race to determine who can and who can't live on certain property. The author claims this ruling is "justly celebrated." *However*, the author fears the reasoning behind the ruling is *problematic*. This problem will serve as the **Scope** of the passage. The author's **Purpose** will likely be to explain or describe this problem.

The second paragraph presents the basis for the ruling: the Fourteenth Amendment, which requires that states give all citizens equal protection. *But*, the author raises a question. If the amendment applies to state actions, why did the Court use it to rule on a private issue? The author then provides the Court's reasoning, which will surely be questioned later based on the author's earlier assessment of this reasoning as problematic. The Court claimed that the private covenants themselves were legal, but the *enforcement* of them wasn't, because enforcement is a state action. Essentially, states can't enforce a rule that discriminates based on race, as that would violate the Fourteenth Amendment.

In the third paragraph, as expected, the author points out a flaw in this logic. By this reasoning, all private agreements would inevitably turn into state issues whenever individuals seek judicial enforcement—which is all the time. Thus, there would be no real distinction between private and state matters. According to the author, this is the primary reason courts don't use this reasoning anymore. As an example, the author mentions how courts will now enforce private agreements that limit free speech, even though state laws limiting free speech would be unconstitutional.

In the final paragraph, the author raises one more problem with the ruling. Lest it be forgotten, the Court actually claimed that the covenants themselves were legal. According to the author, this indicates the Court completely ignored the actual problem of how discriminatory the covenants are.

The last three paragraphs essentially expand upon and support the ideas expressed in the first paragraph. So, the **Main Idea** is, while the ruling in *Shelley v. Kraemer* is justifiably praised, the reasoning behind that ruling is ultimately flawed.

1. (A) Global

Step 2: Identify the Question Type
The question asks for the "primary purpose" of the entire passage, making this a Global question.

Step 3: Research the Relevant Text
As the question asks about the entire passage, all of the text is relevant. There's no need to go back into the passage itself.

The overall purpose was predicted when summarizing the big picture.

Step 4: Make a Prediction
The author's purpose was to discuss the problems in the reasoning behind the *Shelley v. Kraemer* ruling.

Step 5: Evaluate the Answer Choices
(A) is correct.

(B) is a Faulty Use of Detail. This distinction is discussed throughout the second and third paragraph, but only as part of the explanation why the ruling in question was problematic. The author's focus is solely on that ruling, not the way law works in general.

(C) is Out of Scope. There is no discussion of how scholars explain the ruling.

(D) is a Distortion. The author doesn't question the Constitution itself. The author only argues that one amendment was misused in a particular ruling.

(E) is Out of Scope and a 180. The author is only focused on the one case. Besides, in the third paragraph, the author claims that the rationale was *not* extended to other cases. Courts no longer apply it.

2. (B) Logic Reasoning (Evaluate the Argument)

Step 2: Identify the Question Type
This asks for a question that would be "most relevant" in making a determination. This is similar to what Evaluate the Argument questions ask in Logical Reasoning. In this case, the correct answer will question whether or not one can conclude that an unspecified action is considered a "state action" based on the information given in the passage about such actions.

Step 3: Research the Relevant Text
The question refers to line 19, but be sure to read the surrounding lines for context.

Step 4: Make a Prediction
The phrase "state action" is said to be what's necessary to invoke the Fourteenth Amendment. This phrase refers back to lines 7–8, which claim the amendment applies to "state actors but not individuals." So, to conclude that something is a "state action," it must be determined whether the action is being performed by the state or by an individual. The correct answer should raise the question of who's performing the action.

Step 5: Evaluate the Answer Choices
(B) is correct.

(A) is a Distortion. Calling it a "state action" is based on who is performing the action (is it the state or not?), not who is affected by the action.

(C) is Out of Scope. The designation of "state action" is based on who performs the action, not any principle underlying the action.

(D) is a Distortion. Whether an action is called a "state action" depends on the people performing the action, not those affected by the action.

(E) is Out of Scope. The designation of an action as a "state action" is based on *who* performs the action, not *why* they perform the action.

3. (E) Inference

Step 2: Identify the Question Type
The question asks for a phrase that indicates the "author's attitude," making this an Inference question. Unlike most Inference questions, though, the correct answer will consist of text lifted directly from the passage.

Step 3: Research the Relevant Text
The author's attitude is present throughout the passage, so don't go looking for one phrase in particular, as there could be too many to choose from. Instead, predict the author's general attitude and test the answer choices individually, *in context*, to match that general idea.

Step 4: Make a Prediction
The question asks for the author's attitude toward the Court's reasoning, which the author professed at the beginning as *problematic* (line 13). The correct answer will be a phrase from the passage that indicates this perception of the reasoning as problematic.

Step 5: Evaluate the Answer Choices
(E) is correct. This is the author's description of a particular problem, as detailed in the last paragraph. Even if you couldn't define the word *noxious* exactly, it's used to describe an aspect of the reasoning that the author claims "fails to target" the real issue, and is thus problematic.

(A) is a Distortion. This suggests that the ruling is famous for what it accomplished, but does nothing to indicate the author's problem with the reasoning behind the ruling.

(B) is a Distortion. This indicates the author's attitude toward the ultimate ruling. However, the question asks for the author's attitude on the *reasoning* behind the ruling, not the ruling itself. While the author does approve of the ruling, the author's attitude is less glowing about the reasoning behind the ruling, which is said to be *problematic*.

(C) is a Faulty Use of Detail. This describes the Court's opinion about the covenants, not the author's opinion about the Court's reasoning.

(D) is a Distortion. This refers to the hypothetical result of applying the reasoning consistently to other cases. This does not indicate the author's negative attitude toward the reasoning, and fails to account for the fact that the author

later says this reasoning is *not* consistently applied anymore, as courts have stopped using it.

4. (C) Logic Reasoning (Parallel Reasoning)

Step 2: Identify the Question Type
The question asks for a situation that is "most analogous" to the ideas expressed in the passage. That makes this a Parallel Reasoning question, similar to those found in Logical Reasoning.

Step 3: Research the Relevant Text
The question refers to the word *attribution* in line 28, but that is preceded immediately by the word *this*, which refers to the description of attribution in the previous sentence.

Step 4: Make a Prediction
The phrase "this attribution" refers to the reasoning in lines 25–27, in which the responsibility for private provisions are shifted over to the state when courts are asked to enforce them. In short, *attribution* refers to the shift in responsibility from the individual (private) to a larger collective (the state). The correct answer will apply that same logic to another issue.

Step 5: Evaluate the Answer Choices
(C) is correct, showing how responsibility for something (in this case, an op-ed piece) can shift from the individual (the columnist who wrote it) to a larger collective (the newspaper that publishes it).

(A) is a Distortion. This puts responsibility on the group at fault without attributing it (or shifting responsibility) to a large collective.

(B) is a Distortion. This does not shift the responsibility, as attribution would. Instead, the individual is always held accountable.

(D) is a Distortion. This places responsibility only on the individual without attributing it to a larger collective.

(E) is a Distortion. This places responsibility on a collective (the company), but the collective always had the responsibility. It wasn't attributed (or shifted) from any individual.

5. (B) Logic Function

Step 2: Identify the Question Type
The phrase "in order to" at the end indicates the question is asking *why* the author asks the given question, making this a Logic Function question.

Step 3: Research the Relevant Text
The quoted text comes from the second paragraph. Be sure to consider the entire context of the paragraph as well as the passage as a whole, and not just the quote itself.

Step 4: Make a Prediction

The author's purpose in the second paragraph is to introduce the Court's reasoning, which the author has already described as *problematic*. The author goes on to question this reasoning in the subsequent paragraphs. The quote in question raises a particular issue that is discussed throughout the second and third paragraphs: If the covenants are part of private contracts, how did the Court consider this a state action? This question serves as the basis for the author's complaints against the reasoning of the Court's decision.

Step 5: Evaluate the Answer Choices

(B) is correct. It is a potentially confusing issue (as the Court took a private matter and somehow turned it into a state matter), and it is central to the author's argument against the reasoning behind the Court's decision.

(A) is a Distortion. By the third paragraph, the author does claim that the case could dissolve the distinction between private and state actions. However, the author never claims that distinction is "conceptually incoheren[t]." The concept is fine. The Court just failed to use it properly.

(C) is Out of Scope. The author never questions the facts of the case or how those facts were used.

(D) is Out of Scope. The author only addresses the Court as a whole, not the individual judges.

(E) is a Distortion. The author is questioning the Court's application of the Fourteenth Amendment, not the amendment itself.

6. (D) Logic Reasoning (Principle)

Step 2: Identify the Question Type

The question directly asks for a *principle* the author uses, making this a Principle question like those found in Logical Reasoning.

Step 3: Research the Relevant Text

The author's argument is spread throughout the passage, so there's no one specific area that can be targeted as relevant.

Step 4: Make a Prediction

The author's argument is that the reasoning behind the ruling is problematic. So, any principle should revolve around making such an assessment. Furthermore, the assessment should be based on any of the various arguments the author makes in the third and fourth paragraphs. There are several to choose from, so it would be better to use the choices to research rather than making multiple predictions, most of which will wind up going unused.

Step 5: Evaluate the Answer Choices

(D) is correct, providing a principle to assess a court's reasoning (rationale) as problematic (questionable). This bases the assessment on whether courts are hesitant to apply rationales from previous decisions. That's one of the author's arguments in the third paragraph (lines 44–46), where the author claims that courts no longer apply the rationale behind the *Shelley v. Kraemer* decision.

(A) is Out of Scope. There is no mention of legal scholars or their assessment of the Court's rationale.

(B) is Out of Scope and a Distortion. There is no mention of private agreements being "judicially unenforceable." Besides, this provides no basis for the author's argument about the problematic nature of the reasoning behind the ruling.

(C) is a Distortion. The author does provide evidence of the Court's failure to address the genuine problem (lines 57–59), but the author never goes so far as to recommend taking measures to stop that problem. The author is only concerned with revealing the flaws in the Court's reasoning.

(E) is Out of Scope and a Distortion. The author never describes the rationale as *controversial*. Further, the author never advocates for a new rationale. If the rationale given in a judicial decision is found to be controversial, the decision should be supported by offering a new rationale.

Passage 2: Did the Botai Ride Horses?

Step 1: Read the Passage Strategically
Sample Roadmap

line #	Keyword/phrase	¶ Margin notes
3	may	Olsen: evid of horse domest/riding
5	momentous	
9–10	not immediately evident	Bones could be wild or domestic
11	because	
13	So	
14	relies heavily	Olsen uses stats
20	typically	Domesticated: usually kill most males, keep females
23	however	
25	One might suppose	But Botai horses - lots of adult males
29	However	
30	:	Wild and hunted?
34	so	
36	Thus	Olsen: if hunted, less adult males
37	argues	
38	But	
40	?; reasons	Why males not killed young?
43	Another clue	Olsen: kept for riding
47	unreasonable	Add'l evid: full skeletons, too big to drag
49	reasons	
55	further suggests; beyond	buried carefully indicates significance
56	merely	

Discussion

The author begins by introducing Sandra Olsen, an archaeologist who may have found the earliest known evidence of something the author declares *momentous*: humans domesticating and riding horses. The evidence is a large portion of horse bones found in a once inhabited area of Kazhakstan. The bones themselves are not enough to show domestication, as the bones of wild and domesticated horses are pretty much the same. So, Olsen relies on statistics to bolster her claim that these horses were domesticated. The **Topic** of the passage is Olsen's discovery of the horse bones, while the **Scope** focuses on Olsen's claim that these bones indicate the earliest known domestication and riding of horses. With the mention of Olsen's use of statistics to defend her view, the **Purpose** of the passage is likely to present and explain the statistics Olsen uses to support her view.

As expected, the second paragraph presents some of Olsen's statistics. At first glance, Olsen's statistics seem to contradict her view. It's claimed that most of the male horses Olsen found were fully grown and that these males outnumbered the females. However, this goes against the norms of domestication, as males are usually killed off before they mature. Further, it seems to suggest the horses were actually wild, as hunters of wild animals would usually prefer large adult males. However, Olsen defends her position by claiming that horses are different. First, she addresses the hunting issue. Wild horses are usually found in either large families of predominantly female horses or random scatterings of male bachelors. Clustered families would make easier targets. So, if the horses were actually wild and hunted, one would expect to find more female bones, not male bones. And the fact that herders usually kill males before they mature? Olsen has an answer for that, too: The males could have been kept alive for riding.

The third paragraph provides more evidence for domestication. The bones Olsen found were mostly full skeletons. Horses, she argues, are a bit too large to have been hunted and dragged back home in one piece. Further, the skeletons were buried and arranged carefully, suggesting that the horses were viewed as something more than just food.

It's easy to get caught up in all of the details in the second and third paragraphs. However, it's more important to note that everything in those paragraphs is there to support the **Main Idea** presented at the very beginning: Based on her statistical analysis, Olsen claims that the bones she found in Kazakhstan offer evidence of the earliest known instance of domesticating and riding horses.

7. (C) Global

Step 2: Identify the Question Type
The question asks for the "main point" of the entire passage, making this a Global question.

Step 3: Research the Relevant Text
As with any Global question, the entire text is relevant. Instead of going back into the passage, use the Main Idea as predicted while formulating the big picture.

Step 4: Make a Prediction
The Main Idea of the passage is that Olsen argues the bones she found in Kazakhstan provide evidence for the earliest known instance of horse domestication and riding.

Step 5: Evaluate the Answer Choices
(C) is correct, describing Olsen's use of evidence to support the claim of domestication and riding.

(A) is a Distortion. The author is not making some grand claim about the use of statistics in the field of archaeology as a whole. The passage is focused solely on Olsen's work on this one particular subject of horse domestication and riding.

(B) is a Distortion. Olsen's analysis is meant to indicate the Botai are notable if they provide evidence of the first domestication and riding of horses. Olsen's interest in them is not whether horses simply played a *critical* role in the Botai culture.

(D) is Extreme and a Distortion. The author claims that Olsen's findings *may* be evidence of domestication (lines 3–4), and thus never claims they are conclusive. Further, while the author does claim that domestication was part of a momentous development, it fails to account for the other development: riding. Furthermore, Olsen's findings are only meant to show whether domestication and riding occurred, not whether those developments were actually momentous.

(E) is a Distortion. The author never discusses any human remains from the site, and Olsen only claims the horses were domesticated and ridden, not *revered*.

8. (B) Inference

Step 2: Identify the Question Type
The question asks for the "author's attitude," which is a regularly tested variation of an Inference question.

Step 3: Research the Relevant Text
The second and third paragraphs are mostly filled with statistics and details, so any author attitude would be inferred primarily from the first paragraph.

Step 4: Make a Prediction
The author never makes any outright declarations about Olsen's views. However, the author does claim in the first paragraph that her findings "may be evidence" of something the author regards as momentous. And the author never

rejects any of her claims. So, if anything, by devoting three paragraphs to Olsen's opinions, the author provides some modicum of support, even if it's not explicit.

Step 5: Evaluate the Answer Choices

(B) is correct, suggesting that the author's endorsement is merely implied and not directly stated.

(A) is Extreme. The author never goes so far as to advocate for Olsen's views, and is never truly forthright with any strong opinions one way or the other.

(C) is a Distortion. The author calls domestication a "momentous development," which suggests the author is hardly ambivalent about the subject matter.

(D) is a 180. The author does raise some questions in the second paragraph. However, they are not asked to indicate skepticism. Instead, the author is anticipating arguments and raising those questions to show how Olsen already has answers for them. There's no suggestion that the author has any doubts about her responses.

(E) is a 180. The author never expresses any negativity toward Olsen or her views.

9. (E) Inference

Step 2: Identify the Question Type

The question essentially asks for the implied meaning of the word *beyond*, making this a vocab-in-context form of Inference question.

Step 3: Research the Relevant Text

The word in question is on line 55, but it's important to read around that line to understand the context fully.

Step 4: Make a Prediction

The full sentence goes from lines 52 to 56, and the author is discussing how the horse skeletons were found buried and carefully arranged. This, according to the author, suggests a relationship to horses "beyond that of merely hunting." The careful burial suggests that the horses were not just dumped aside when they died. They were not just hunted for food. The relationship was deeper than that. In other words, it was more than just a hunter-food relationship. The correct answer should describe how *beyond* means "more than."

Step 5: Evaluate the Answer Choices

(E) is correct, as it is the only one that suggests a relationship that involves *more* than just hunter and prey.

(A) is a 180. Calling the relationship *parallel* to the hunter-food relationship suggests similarity, and the author is suggesting these horses were treated differently—in a more special manner.

(B) is a 180. These people seemed to have achieved the kind of relationship that would lead to such a careful burial of the horses. There's no evidence that such a relationship would be elusive.

(C) is Out of Scope. There's nothing to suggest that anyone would find it difficult to understand the relationship these people had with their horses.

(D) is Out of Scope. There's nothing necessarily unclear about the relationship being suggested: The horses were domesticated, ridden, and perhaps seen as pets or like part of the family, not just as food.

10. (C) Inference

Step 2: Identify the Question Type

This question provides a hypothetical situation and asks for something for which that situation would "provide evidence." In other words, the hypothetical situation would support what the correct answer says, making this an Inference question.

Step 3: Research the Relevant Text

The hypothetical situation discusses the gender makeup of the bones, which relates to the gender concepts raised throughout the second paragraph.

Step 4: Make a Prediction

The question asks what could be hypothesized if the bones were mostly fully grown females and young males. This would conform perfectly to what herders typically do with domesticated animals: keep the females but kill off most of the males before they mature (lines 19–21). So, the correct answer will likely suggest the horses were domesticated.

Step 5: Evaluate the Answer Choices

(C) is correct, indicating domestication as predicted. But what about the riding part? That refers back to the end of the second paragraph. In the actual findings, Olsen found a lot of mature males, which she suggests indicated that the Botai kept the males alive to ride them. So, if the males had been all young (as this question asks), then the Botai probably weren't riding them.

(A) is a 180. If the Botai had been targeting males when hunting, they'd probably be looking for bigger, mature males (lines 27–29), not young males, as this question asks.

(B) is a 180 on multiple accounts. If there were mostly females and young males, that's more consistent with domesticated animals, not wild animals. Furthermore, riding horses would be done with adult males, not young males.

(D) is Out of Scope. By lines 19–21, the presence of a lot of females and young males would be consistent with herding animals for food. There's no suggestion of other sources of food.

(E) is Out of Scope. There is no information in the passage that suggests anything about cultural rituals.

11. (D) Inference

Step 2: Identify the Question Type
The question asks for something about which the author is "most likely to agree," making this an Inference question.

Step 3: Research the Relevant Text
The question provides no line references or Content Clues, so the entire passage is relevant.

Step 4: Make a Prediction
With no clues to work with, a prediction will be impossible here. Instead, test the answer choices based on what's consistent with the big picture. Be wary of choices that seem to be strongly worded or contain outside information.

Step 5: Evaluate the Answer Choices
(D) is correct. From the bones Olsen found at the site, she could really only determine whether they were male or female. To support her interpretation that this indicated domestication and riding, she used all sorts of outside facts about herding and hunting patterns, as described throughout the second paragraph.

(A) is Extreme. While Olsen used mortality patterns to support her view, there's nothing to suggest developing such patterns is *always* required.

(B) is Extreme and Out of Scope. While the author does suggest that Olsen's findings aren't conclusive, that doesn't have to be because she didn't corroborate her view with evidence from another site. And there's no suggestion that such corroboration is really necessary.

(C) is Extreme and Out of Scope. The passage is only concerned about whether the Botai domesticated and rode horses, not whether they reached a "high level of social organization." Moreover, even if they did, that's not to say that *any* culture that carefully arranges bones would be reaching any particular level.

(E) is Out of Scope. The author never addresses how easy it is to domesticate any animal, let alone which ones are easier than others.

12. (A) Logic Function

Step 2: Identify the Question Type
The phrase "serves primarily as" indicates that this is a Logic Function question.

Step 3: Research the Relevant Text
The question asks about the discussion of herding at the beginning of the second paragraph. Be sure to consider the context of the paragraph as a whole—not just what lines 19–21 say.

Step 4: Make a Prediction
The entire second paragraph provides general details about hunting and herding that Olsen uses and addresses to

support her view about the Botai horses being domesticated and ridden. The discussion of herding at the beginning is part of that—statistical patterns that Olsen uses in her argument that the Botai horses were domesticated and ridden.

Step 5: Evaluate the Answer Choices
(A) is correct. Olsen compares the Botai horses to typical herding techniques to draw her conclusion.

(B) is a Distortion and a 180. Lines 19–21 describe what's typical of herders in general. There is no specific example, and this *is* the accepted norm for domesticated animals, not something inconsistent with the norm.

(C) is Out of Scope. While the author does mention goat herding as a general idea, there is no indication that the Botai, in particular, took part in goat herding or that there are any particular beliefs or assumptions about their goat herding (if it existed).

(D) is Out of Scope. This does provide a simple rule of herding domesticated animals. However, the only hypothesis in the passage is about the Botai horses being domesticated and ridden. There's no hypothesis about human-animal relationships in general.

(E) is a Distortion. Olsen does compare the Botai horse population to what's described in lines 19–21. However, there are two problems with this choice. First, the situations are not analogical. Lines 19–21 would result in killing off young males, while the Botai horses contained a lot of adult males. Second, that Botai horses were domesticated and ridden is a hypothesis, not a known fact.

13. (D) Global

Step 2: Identify the Question Type
This question asks for the organization of the entire passage, making this a Global question.

Step 3: Research the Relevant Text
There is no need to go back into the passage itself. Instead, look over the margin notes and focus on the general structure of the passage.

Step 4: Make a Prediction
The first paragraph introduces Olsen's view about the Botai domesticating and riding horses. The second and third paragraphs are filled with her support for that view. The correct answer should indicate that basic structure.

Step 5: Evaluate the Answer Choices
(D) is correct.

(A) is a Distortion. The passage is focused on only one explanation (not "various explanations") for the findings: that they indicate domestication and riding.

(B) reverses the order of the passage, which provides a conclusion first, *then* provides support. Furthermore, there is no stated number of observations.

(C) is a Distortion. Olsen's view is not a general principle. It's a specific hypothesis about the Botai horses.

(E) is Out of Scope. The passage does offer Olsen's proposition at the beginning. However, the rest of the passage is her evidence for that proposition. There is no argument against her.

14. (A) Logic Reasoning (Evaluate the Argument)

Step 2: Identify the Question Type

The question asks for something that would be "most relevant to evaluating" Olsen's hypothesis. That makes this an Evaluate the Argument question, similar to those found in the Logical Reasoning section.

Step 3: Research the Relevant Text

The correct answer will be based on using Olsen's argument, including her hypothesis and the supporting evidence. That's the entire passage. So, everything is relevant to this question.

Step 4: Make a Prediction

Olsen's hypothesis is that the Botai domesticated and rode their horses. This is supported by all of the evidence in the second and third paragraph, including the gender makeup of the group and the careful burial of the bones. Olsen does a great job of providing evidence that supports her view. However, couldn't there be some overlooked evidence that suggests the animals were not domesticated and ridden? Maybe they were wild and hunted? To further evaluate Olsen's argument, the correct answer should provide another way to determine whether the horses were domesticated and ridden or wild and hunted.

Step 5: Evaluate the Answer Choices

(A) is correct. If most of the horses were butchered, then that could question Olsen's view that the Botai tamed and rode these horses. However, if the bones were untouched, then that would suggest the horses were not used for food, and thus more likely to be domesticated, as Olsen claims.

(B) is an Irrelevant Comparison. It doesn't matter what other animals, or how many, were also found at the site. That does nothing to determine how the horses were used.

(C) is an Irrelevant Comparison. The number of other tribes, either contemporary with the Botai or more modern, does nothing to evaluate a hypothesis about the horses.

(D) is Out of Scope. Analyzing other animals will not necessarily shed any light on how the Botai used horses.

(E) is an Irrelevant Comparison. The human-to-horse ratio would not help indicate what the horses were used for. Even if just ceremonial sites were used, that wouldn't help evaluate an argument about horse usage overall.

Passage 3: The Effect of Combining Music and Words

Step 1: Read the Passage Strategically
Sample Roadmap

line #	Keyword/phrase	¶ Margin notes
Passage A		
1	not always	
3	but; inadequate	
4	more adequate; hence	music > words for emotion
9	But	
10	striking effect	Mixing music and words lessens both emotionally
11	but at the expense	
12	But	
13	greater alone	
14	although; good	
16	subordinated	If combined, music should be primary
18	So too; largely	
19	depends; not upon	Examples
21	but upon	
Passage B		
23	two fundamental	
24	:	Two types of opera
28	undeserved contempt	
30	depend	
32	albeit the most important	
33	Theoretically; should be a third	Third type possible, but limited appeal
41	should be judged	Au: to judge opera, consider music and poetry
42	not if	
43	but if	
45	Similarly	
46	not because; but primarily	Music and poetry support each other
49	True	
50	but only	
51	In actuality	combination provides character
55	inimitable	

Discussion

The author of passage A jumps right into the **Topic** (music and words) and **Scope** (their ability to express emotions). The author is very opinionated, arguing music's superiority over words in expressing emotions. Words can excite emotions, but cannot express them adequately. But, set those words to music? Music will take those emotions and express them so deeply that they excite even deeper emotions. Behold the power of music.

But, in the second paragraph, the author expresses a distaste for mixing music and words. It may produce some interesting results, but it dilutes the power of each art form; they work better on their own. If the two are combined, then music—the more emotionally expressive of the two—should be predominant. The author provides examples to support this. Beethoven's *Fifth Symphony* needs no words, and operas have words but ultimately rely more on emotions, which are predominantly expressed by the music. This solidifies the author's **Purpose** (evaluate music v. words) and **Main Idea** (music is superior to words for expressing emotions).

The author of passage B has a more specific **Topic**: opera. The first paragraph of passage B is mostly details about two types of operas: operas in which music is primary (exemplified by Italian operas) and operas in which music mixes with other factors (exemplified by Wagnerian operas). The author admits to a third possible type in which music is secondary, but states such operas were abandoned early on due to a lack of appeal. They needed more music.

The **Scope** of the passage finally shows up in the second paragraph: how to judge operas aesthetically. The author's **Purpose** is to suggest the correct approach. The author argues that the music and poetry of an opera need to be judged together, not individually. The music needs to be seen as serving the story, while the poetry needs to provide an opportunity for musical support. The author admits that they *can* be studied separately, but only for formal analysis. However, it's the combination of music and poetry that defines an opera. That's the author's **Main Idea**.

Both passages focus on the same topic: the combination of music and words. However, passage A focuses on the emotional effect of these arts in general, while passage B focuses on their aesthetic roles, specifically in opera (although passage A does address opera at the end). Further, the author of passage A gives far more weight to music, while the author of passage B gives music and words equal weight.

15. (D) Global

Step 2: Identify the Question Type

This asks for a question that both passages, as a whole, attempt to answer. As the correct answer will be based on overall themes from the passages, this is a Global question.

However, it's important to note that the correct answer need not be a *main* point, as most Global questions would demand.

Step 3: Research the Relevant Text

Without any Content Clues or line references, the entire text is relevant. Focus on the big picture of each passage.

Step 4: Make a Prediction

Both passages are concentrated on the relative roles of music and words when combined. The most prominent common ground between both passages is the effect of music and words in opera. The correct answer is most likely to address that particular concept.

Step 5: Evaluate the Answer Choices

(D) is correct. Although this choice doesn't mention music, it does question the role of words, and both authors do address how words factor into opera.

(A) is only an issue in passage A. Passage B only considers the aesthetic effects of music v. poetry, not their relative ability to be expressive.

(B) is only discussed in passage A. Passage B does not discuss emotions.

(C) is Out of Scope. Passage B does not discuss classical music at all. And the example of Beethoven in passage A is not presented to question which form of music deserves more respect.

(E) is Out of Scope. Passage B only talks about opera, while passage A does not make any distinction between opera and other musical forms.

16. (C) Detail

Step 2: Identify the Question Type

The question asks for something *addressed* in passage A, which means it will be directly presented. That makes this a Detail question. In addition, the correct answer will not be addressed in passage B.

Step 3: Research the Relevant Text

There are no Content Clues or line references, so the entire text is relevant. Use the big picture of both passages to narrow down the choices, and only research individual choices as necessary.

Step 4: Make a Prediction

Both passages are based on the same basic subject matter, so any distinction will come down to different scopes. Unlike passage B, passage A focuses more on the emotional effect of music and words. So, it's likely that the correct answer will hinge on some emotional component of one, if not both, of these art forms.

Step 5: Evaluate the Answer Choices

(C) is correct. The emotional effect of music is described throughout passage A, especially in the first paragraph, while passage B never raises the concept of emotion.

(A) is a 180. The role of music (as well as poetry) in aesthetically judging opera is the entire focus of passage B, not just passage A.

(B) is a 180. This is discussed in passage A, but passage B also talks about the effect of combining music with words, arguing that such combination is what gives opera its character.

(D) is a 180. The author of passage B does mention what happens when music is subordinated (lines 33–38), and the last paragraph essentially suggests that opera wouldn't have its character if music were merely subordinate.

(E) is a 180, as passage B directly addresses whether music and libretto should be judged in isolation (lines 40–41: they shouldn't be).

17. (E) Detail

Step 2: Identify the Question Type

The question asks for something that passage B (and not passage A) directly *includes*, making this a Detail question.

Step 3: Research the Relevant Text

The question asks for a detail about opera, which is unfortunately discussed throughout the entirety of passage B. Thus, the whole passage is relevant. However, for comparison, passage A only really talks about opera in lines 18–22, so consider those lines, too.

Step 4: Make a Prediction

Passage B contains a lot of details about opera, but the question asks for something that wouldn't be in passage A. The common ground for both passages is the effect of combining music and words. That's mostly the second paragraph of passage B. It's the first paragraph of passage B, which goes into the different types of operas, that is mostly distinct from passage A. Expect the correct answer to come from that paragraph.

Step 5: Evaluate the Answer Choices

(E) is correct. Passage B discusses the different types in the first paragraph, while passage A makes no mention of different opera types.

(A) is a 180. The author of passage A *does* mention the aesthetic role of plot and scenery in lines 19–21. It's not an important role, but the author does mention it.

(B) is a 180, as this is explicitly discussed in lines 2–4 of passage A.

(C) is a 180, as passage A directly addresses this in lines 9–16.

(D) is a 180, as this is mentioned in passage A in lines 18–22.

18. (D) Inference

Step 2: Identify the Question Type

The question asks for something that can be *inferred* in the passage, making this an Inference question.

Step 3: Research the Relevant Text

The question refers to passage B, specifically about when words are subordinated to music. That refers to the first type of opera described in lines 24–25 ("music is primary") and then expanded upon in lines 26–29.

Step 4: Make a Prediction

Opera in which words are subordinated is merely one type of opera. The author of passage B does not favor it over other types. In fact, in lines 39–41, the author claims that aesthetic judgment should be consistent for all operas, "regardless of ... type." So, the correct answer should be consistent with this idea that music-dominated operas should be treated just the same as any other opera. They're not special.

Step 5: Evaluate the Answer Choices

(D) is correct, expressing the idea that music-dominated operas need not be treated differently from other operas.

(A) is Extreme and Out of Scope. The author does not discuss the popularity of opera as an art form, and nothing indicates that its popularity serves as its *primary* characteristic.

(B) is a 180 at worst. The author never mentions the "main objectives" of opera. Besides, the only criticism of such operas is mentioned in lines 26–28, in which there is contempt for calling them "singer's opera." However, even that criticism is said to be *un*justified.

(C) is Out of Scope for passage B. The author of passage A would likely agree with this claim, but the author of passage B never discusses the emotional aspect of opera.

(E) is a 180. In lines 42–45, the author argues that operas should *not* be judged as merely a concert piece. The music should be seen as a contribution to the opera's story.

19. (A) Logic Reasoning (Principle)

Step 2: Identify the Question Type

The question asks directly for a principle, making this a Principle question like those found in the Logical Reasoning section. In this case, the principle will be consistent with the ideas in passage B but be contradicted by the ideas in passage A.

Step 3: Research the Relevant Text

The question does not refer to any particular portion of the passages, so the entire text is relevant. Use the big picture to make a prediction here.

Step 4: Make a Prediction

The argument in passage B is that music and words are equally important, which is contradictory to passage A's "it's all about the music" theme. Thus, passage B would follow any principle that allows words *and* music to be equally important, an idea that would certainly be rejected by passage A.

Step 5: Evaluate the Answer Choices

(A) is correct. If an opera can depend on nonmusical elements, then that conforms to the idea in passage B about giving equal weight to the poetry and libretto, while contradicting passage A in its insistence that music is the only thing that matters.

(B) is a 180. This contradicts the author of passage B, who feels that music and other elements should be evaluated together. Instead, this is much more consistent with the thinking behind passage A.

(C) is a Distortion. Operas don't have to be perfectly balanced, according to passage B. It's fine if the words are subordinated by the music. Further, passage A is more concerned with emotional impact than artistic success, so the author of that passage would have no reason to reject this claim.

(D) is a 180. This suggests that music is most important, an idea that passage A would support, not reject.

(E) is Out of Scope for passage A. The author of passage B does suggest this in lines 49–51. However, while the author of passage A clearly favors the musical component of opera, there's no evidence that the author would reject the idea of analyzing the libretto independently.

20. (E) Detail

Step 2: Identify the Question Type

The question asks for a definition given directly in the passage, making this a Detail question.

Step 3: Research the Relevant Text

The phrase "singer's opera" appears in line 27, in the section discussing the different types of operas. Be sure to read around that line for context.

Step 4: Make a Prediction

The "singer's opera" is said to describe the *former* type of opera, i.e., the first of two types listed in the previous sentence. Going back, that refers to the type in which "music is primary."

Step 5: Evaluate the Answer Choices

(E) is correct. If nonmusical elements are subordinate, that's another way of saying that the music elements are predominant, or primary.

(A) is a 180. This describes the second type of opera, referred to as the "latter" type in line 29.

(B) is Out of Scope. There is no mention of a particular type of opera in which the drama is primary.

(C) is a 180. In lines 39–41, judgment should be held "regardless of the opera's type." There's no reason a "singer's opera" should inherently be lower in merit.

(D) is a 180. The earliest operas are mentioned in lines 35–38, and those are said to be a completely different kind in which music is subordinated.

21. (B) Inference

Step 2: Identify the Question Type

The question asks how the author of passage A is "most likely to regard" something mentioned in passage B. That makes this an Inference question.

Step 3: Research the Relevant Text

The question refers to the discussion of the opera type described in lines 33–38. After looking those lines over, consider whether they seem consistent with or contrary to the points made in passage A.

Step 4: Make a Prediction

Lines 33–38 refer to a type of opera in which music is secondary, with other features being primary. It's said that these operas had limited appeal and that operas needed to bulk up on music in order to succeed. This perfectly aligns with the views of passage A's author, who would certainly take this as evidence that music is really important.

Step 5: Evaluate the Answer Choices

(B) is correct.

(A) is Extreme and a Distortion. While the author of passage A does believe this, the lack of interest in music-subordinate operas does not necessarily indicate that the music and the poetry were *both* diminished. Perhaps the poetry was fine, but only the music suffered.

(C) is a Faulty Use of Detail. The indivisibility of musical and nonmusical elements is a passage B idea (lines 51–55), not a passage A idea.

(D) is a 180. These operas lacked appeal. There is no gain. Besides, this would completely contradict passage A's insistence that music is better alone than with words (lines 12–14).

(E) is a 180. The author of passage A does not feel that all elements are equal. The author of passage A argues that music is most important.

Passage 4: Subduction and Earthquake Frequency

Step 1: Read the Passage Strategically
Sample Roadmap

line #	Keyword/phrase	¶ Margin notes
1	generally accepted	General theory: plates collide, causes earthquakes
9	Acccording to	
14	Contrary to expectations	But, some subduction areas have fewer earthquakes
15	however	
17–18	nonetheless; Thus, until recently; crucial question	
19	no answer	Why?
21	?	
22	proposes	Scientists: depends on collision type
27	because	Hot zones: opposite direction
29–30	In contrast	Quiet zones: same direction
34	But	
37	Thus	↑ subduction depth, ↓ contact, ↓ earthquakes
44	On the other hand	↓ subduction depth, ↑ contact, ↑ earthquakes
52	warning	Warning: risk of earthquakes even if subduction is low

Discussion

This passage is bound to intimidate anybody who takes a quick glance and gets nervous about the abundance of scientific jargon (e.g., plate tectonics, subduction, seismic data). However, it's important to remember that the LSAT is not testing scientific knowledge. Simplify the language and focus instead on the broader ideas and the major opinions.

The passage opens up with details about how earthquakes happen. (That indicates earthquakes are the **Topic** of this passage.) The earth's crust is made up of plates that move around. When two plates crash into each other, one is forced under the other, and this is called *subduction*. This process causes a lot of energy to build up, which results in earthquakes. And most earthquakes occur where subduction is pretty common ("hot zones"). [*H*]owever, lines 14–21 are where things get interesting. There are some areas where plates collide often but *don't* produce earthquakes. This raises the question at the end of the paragraph: Why don't these areas get a lot of earthquakes? The author claims this has been a question "until recently" (lines 17–18), which is a huge hint to the **Scope** of the passage (the question of why high-subduction areas don't get a lot of earthquakes) and the **Purpose** (to provide an answer to that question).

The second paragraph wastes no time getting to the proposed answer. Some scientists claim it's all about *how* the plates collide. In many "hot zones," the plates move toward each other and crash into one another. *In contrast*, the quieter zones have plates moving in the same direction. When two plates collide, one is just moving faster and crashes underneath the slower one in front. This produces less friction and thus fewer earthquakes. That's it. There's a lot more science you could wade through, but the **Main Idea** is settled: Some scientists argue that the way in which plates move can help explain why some high-subduction areas don't get a lot of earthquakes.

The last paragraph provides a quick warning about the implication of this proposal. If it's correct, then even areas that don't have a lot of subduction can still be susceptible to major earthquakes, depending on which way the plates are moving when any subduction does occur.

22. (B) Global

Step 2: Identify the Question Type
The question asks for the "main point of the passage," making this a Global question.

Step 3: Research the Relevant Text
As with any Global question, the entire text is relevant. Instead of going back into the passage, use the Main Idea as predicted while summarizing the big picture.

Step 4: Make a Prediction
The Main Idea is that some scientists now claim that areas with a lot of subduction may not get a lot of earthquakes because of the way in which the plates move.

Step 5: Evaluate the Answer Choices
(B) is correct, as it summarizes how the movement of the plates (either toward each other or in the same direction) can explain why some areas with a lot of subduction don't get a lot of earthquakes.

(A) is a 180, at worst. The proposal discussed in the passage is meant to explain why the amount of subduction does *not* correlate with the number of earthquakes. Some areas with a lot of subduction get a lot of earthquakes, while other high-subduction areas don't.

(C) is a Distortion. The proposal does claim that quiet zones occur when plates are moving in the same direction. However, the plates *do* still collide in quiet zones (lines 29–34), just not in the same earthquake-producing way.

(D) is Extreme and a 180. There is no replacement of the original theory. Earthquakes are *still* said to result from subduction. It's just that not all types of subduction are as prone to earthquakes.

(E) is a Distortion. The proposal does not threaten the accepted theory. Subduction is still the cause of earthquakes. It's just that subduction does not *always* cause earthquakes, and the new theory explains why.

23. (D) Detail

Step 2: Identify the Question Type
The correct answer will be directly stated, "[a]ccording to the passage," making this a Detail question.

Step 3: Research the Relevant Text
The question refers to what happens when two plates collide while moving in the same direction. This is described in lines 29–34 of the second paragraph.

Step 4: Make a Prediction
Lines 29–34 state that when two plates moving in the same direction collide, one is faster than the other and the leading edge of the faster plate is subducted under the slower plate.

Step 5: Evaluate the Answer Choices
(D) matches the details of the passage.

(A) is inaccurate because the faster-moving plate is subducted, not the slower-moving plate.

(B) is also inaccurate because, again, the faster-moving plate is subducted, not the slower-moving plate.

(C) is inaccurate because the leading edge of the faster plate is subducted, not the trailing edge.

(E) is Out of Scope. Subduction depends on the speed of the plates, not the size of the plates.

24. (C) Logic Reasoning (Weaken)

Step 2: Identify the Question Type

The question asks for something that would "present the greatest challenge" to the new proposal, making this a Weaken question like those found in Logical Reasoning.

Step 3: Research the Relevant Text

The new proposal is outlined throughout the second paragraph.

Step 4: Make a Prediction

The gist of the new proposal is that a lot of earthquakes happen when plates are moving toward each other. When plates are moving in the same direction, there aren't as many earthquakes. Any situation that contradicts one (or both) of these cases will provide a challenge to the proposal. Start with that, and be prepared to go back to the passage if choices bring up other minor details.

Step 5: Evaluate the Answer Choices

(C) is correct. The angle of subduction is mentioned in line 40 and lines 47–48. A steep angle of descent occurs when plates are moving in the same direction, which should produce fewer earthquakes. A shallow angle occurs when plates move toward each other, which should produce more earthquakes. If areas with a shallow angle produce very few earthquakes, that would indeed contradict the proposal.

(A) is a 180. This is consistent with the proposal, suggesting that plates moving in the same direction produce fewer earthquakes.

(B) is a 180. The proposal accepts that such areas exist. In fact, the proposal is designed to explain *why* this happens.

(D) is a 180. The details in the second paragraph confirm that different angles produce different sizes of the plane of contact. So, even if the angle was the only factor relevant to the plane of contact, this would still be consistent with the proposal, not contradictory.

(E) is a 180. According to the proposal, a steep angle reduces friction, and thus reduces the potential for earthquakes (lines 40–44). Thus, this is consistent with the proposal, not a challenge to it.

25. (E) Inference

Step 2: Identify the Question Type

The question asks for a sentence that would logically complete the last paragraph. Any logical final sentence would be supported by the information before it, making this an Inference question.

Step 3: Research the Relevant Text

The question asks for something that would come at the very end, so start with the details of the last paragraph to predict where the author would go next.

Step 4: Make a Prediction

In the last paragraph, the author discusses how regions with infrequent subduction could still be at risk of earthquakes. However, it never directly says how. All it says is that it "depend[s] on the nature of the subduction taking place." Using the information from the previous paragraph, earthquakes are more likely to occur when plates are moving toward each other. So, a logical conclusion would say that areas with infrequent subduction could still get earthquakes if the plates there were moving toward each other.

Step 5: Evaluate the Answer Choices

(E) is correct. This does require a little extra research to confirm the details. Shallow angles occur when plates are moving toward each other (lines 44–48), which is what the author is suggesting could cause problems, even in regions where subduction is infrequent.

(A) is a 180. The author is suggesting that there might be a risk of earthquakes, which would supposedly happen when plates are moving toward each other. Velocity only matters when plates are moving in the same direction, not toward each other.

(B) is not supported. There is no suggestion of any proportional relationship between subduction level and angle of subduction.

(C) is a Distortion. The passage is not saying that subduction levels could increase. It's just saying there could always be some risk of earthquakes regardless of the level.

(D) is Extreme and a 180, at worst. This contradicts the second paragraph, which goes to great lengths to explain why some subduction does *not* inevitably produce earthquakes.

26. (C) Detail

Step 2: Identify the Question Type

The question asks for something that is stated "[a]ccording to the information in the passage," making this a Detail question.

Step 3: Research the Relevant Text

The question asks for the type of region most prone to earthquakes. That data is presented in the second paragraph. Specifically, the regions prone to earthquakes are described in lines 24–29 and 44–51.

Step 4: Make a Prediction

The earthquake-prone regions are the ones in which the plates are moving toward each other. According to lines 44–51, the colliding plates experience very little resistance from the mantle, so subduction occurs at a shallow angle. However, there's a large plane of contact between the plates, so the plates experience a lot of resistance from each other. The correct answer will likely utilize one or more of these pieces of data.

Step 5: Evaluate the Answer Choices

(C) is correct, as confirmed in lines 47–48.

(A) is a 180. This describes regions where the plates move in the same direction (lines 38–40), which is where there are fewer earthquakes.

(B) is a 180. The plates in earthquake-prone regions receive little resistance from the mantle (lines 44–47). It's the quiet zones where plates get a lot of resistance from the mantle (lines 38–39).

(D) is also a 180. The point of the second paragraph is that areas with a lot of subduction may *not* experience a lot of earthquakes because of the way the plates move.

(E) is another 180. When plates are moving in the same direction, that's when earthquakes are *less* likely to occur.

27. (E) Inference

Step 2: Identify the Question Type

The question asks for something that "can be inferred," making this an Inference question.

Step 3: Research the Relevant Text

The question asks about seismic activity (i.e., earthquakes), which is discussed throughout the passage. Hence, the entire text is relevant.

Step 4: Make a Prediction

With no real clues to work with, a specific prediction will not be possible. Instead, stick with the general theme of the passage: Plates moving toward each other? Earthquakes likely. Plates moving in the same direction? Earthquakes not so likely. Start there, and test individual choices as necessary.

Step 5: Evaluate the Answer Choices

(E) is correct. This is supported in lines 48–49, which describe regions more prone to earthquakes as experiencing a "larger plane of contact between ... plates."

(A) is Extreme and a 180. Earthquakes are not frequent in *any* zone with colliding plates. In fact, the entire purpose of the second paragraph is to show why some such zones do *not* produce a lot of earthquakes.

(B) is Out of Scope. The author discusses the size of the plane of contact (lines 48–49), but never mentions where along that plane earthquakes are likely to occur.

(C) is a Faulty Use of Detail. This refers to the buildup of energy caused by subduction discussed in lines 9–12. However, there is no evidence that such buildup occurs gradually in quiet zones, and there's no mention that quiet zones are at any particular risk.

(D) is Extreme. While subduction does cause earthquakes, there's nothing to suggest that earthquakes *need* to happen to identify a subduction zone. There could be plenty of other ways to identify subduction that are not addressed by this passage.

Section II: Logical Reasoning

Q#	Question Type	Correct	Difficulty
1	Flaw	A	★
2	Principle (Identify/Strengthen)	B	★
3	Flaw	D	★
4	Principle (Identify/Assumption)	C	★
5	Assumption (Necessary)	B	★
6	Flaw	B	★
7	Strengthen	E	★★
8	Main Point	C	★★★
9	Weaken	A	★★
10	Main Point	A	★★
11	Paradox	D	★
12	Weaken	B	★★
13	Paradox	E	★
14	Strengthen	C	★
15	Flaw	E	★★★
16	Weaken	A	★★★
17	Inference	C	★★★
18	Strengthen	A	★★★★
19	Parallel Reasoning	B	★★
20	Inference	B	★★★
21	Assumption (Sufficient)	A	★★★★
22	Inference	B	★★★★
23	Parallel Flaw	C	★★★★
24	Strengthen	A	★★
25	Role of a Statement	D	★★
26	Strengthen	D	★

LSAT PrepTest 85 Unlocked

1. (A) Flaw

Step 1: Identify the Question Type
The question asks why the given argument is "vulnerable to criticism," making this a Flaw question. As an added bonus, the question stem indicates that the flaw will be something the author "fails to consider."

Step 2: Untangle the Stimulus
Plato argued that societies should restrict music because music can manipulate emotions in a harmful manner. Ullman concludes that this argument is misguided. As evidence, Ullman states that musicians aren't trying to manipulate emotions; they're just trying to create something beautiful.

Step 3: Make a Prediction
Even though musicians aren't *trying* to manipulate emotions, that doesn't mean it isn't happening. Ullman assumes otherwise, overlooking the possibility that harmful manipulation can happen even if it's not the intention of musicians. The correct answer will point out this overlooked distinction.

Step 4: Evaluate the Answer Choices
(A) is correct, suggesting that music can still manipulate emotions even if musicians don't intend it.

(B) is Out of Scope. This argument is not concerned with censoring other forms of expression.

(C) is Out of Scope. Ullman is only disputing Plato's argument. Even if a better argument for censorship exists, Ullman could still claim Plato's argument is unsound.

(D) is an Irrelevant Comparison. The argument is not about how music compares to other art forms. All that matters is whether or not Plato's argument is valid.

(E) is Out of Scope. Ullman did not ask musicians what their intent was. Instead, it was categorically stated musicians are *not* trying to manipulate emotions. So, it's immaterial whether musicians would mislead about their intent, because they were never given an opportunity to do so.

2. (B) Principle (Identify/Strengthen)

Step 1: Identify the Question Type
The question directly asks for a principle, making this an Identify the Principle question. Further, the principle will be used to *justify* a conclusion, which means this question will also use the skills of a Strengthen question.

Step 2: Untangle the Stimulus
The physician concludes that the tax on saturated fat should not have been repealed so quickly. The tax was meant to discourage people from eating unhealthy foods, but it was repealed after just seven months because it was leading to undesirable consequences.

Step 3: Make a Prediction
The physician offers evidence why the tax was repealed (the consequences), but never offers evidence to keep it other than its intention to help people eat better. Note, though, that the physician concludes the repeal shouldn't have happened "so soon." The tax was only in effect for seven months. The physician is thus assuming that seven months was not enough time for the tax plan to work properly. Perhaps the plan needed a little more time to work out the kinks. To justify keeping the tax around longer, the physician must be acting on a principle that plans need sufficient time—at least more than seven months—to do their job.

Step 4: Evaluate the Answer Choices
(B) is correct. If a tax plan needs at least a year to gauge its impact on health, then the physician is justified in claiming that seven months was too quick to take it away.

(A) is Out of Scope. The physician's argument is about whether or not the plan should have been repealed, not whether or not it should have been implemented in the first place.

(C) is Out of Scope. The physician is only concerned with the repeal, not the initial implementation. Besides, the negative consequences are said to be unintended. There's no evidence whether or not they were foreseeable or whether such consequences were considered beforehand.

(D) is Extreme and a 180 at worst. There's no evidence of how many people are evading the law, let alone that it's *most* people. Besides, if most people were evading the law, this would justify repealing the law, not keeping it around.

(E) is Out of Scope. Like **(C)**, **(E)** focuses on what plans should be implemented, but the physician's focus is on the repeal, which was based solely on the negative consequences of the tax plan. The physician's claim that the plan was repealed too soon is not predicated on which foods are impacted by the plan. Furthermore, it's not clear whether saturated fat is considered a food that is the "most unhealthy."

3. (D) Flaw

Step 1: Identify the Question Type
The question asks for a "flaw in the reasoning," making this a Flaw question.

Step 2: Untangle the Stimulus
The legislator argues that the sale of domestic iron-mining company FerroMetal to a foreign company should be prohibited. The evidence is that the legislator's region needs a dependable supply of iron ore. If a foreign company buys FerroMetal, then other foreign companies could come and buy other domestic iron-mining companies, which would lead to foreign companies controlling the iron mining, resulting in the loss of a reliable domestic supply of iron ore.

Step 3: Make a Prediction

This type of argument is often referred to as a "slippery slope." It's based on one thing happening that supposedly will lead to a series of worse and worse events until things go horribly, horribly wrong. The problem is that it's all based on what *could* happen, and the legislator is merely assuming the worst will happen. It's possible that other foreign companies will start buying all the other iron-mining companies and taking over everything. Or ... maybe they won't. The legislator insists on taking the pessimistic view, and the correct answer will expose the legislator's refusal to see other less dire outcomes.

Step 4: Evaluate the Answer Choices

(D) is correct, pointing out the legislator's insistence that the one terrible sequence of events is the only possible outcome.

(A) describes Circular Reasoning, but that doesn't apply here. The conclusion here is that the sale should be prohibited, a recommendation supported by independent (albeit flawed) evidence. There is no mere restatement of evidence.

(B) is Out of Scope. The argument is only concerned with the iron mining industry. The legislator does not apply this logic to other industries in general.

(C) is Out of Scope. There is no evidence that this practice of selling a domestic company is "widely accepted."

(E) is inaccurate. All of the events are presented in the correct chronological order.

4. (C) Principle (Identify/Assumption)

Step 1: Identify the Question Type

The question asks for a principle, making this an Identify the Principle question. Further, the principle will be based on a line of reasoning, i.e., an argument. Thus, this will require breaking an argument into its evidence and conclusion, just as in an Assumption question, although it may not be crucial to actually identify the assumption.

Step 2: Untangle the Stimulus

The engineer is steadfast in concluding that dumping chemicals into the river is okay, despite evidence of potential health problems. To support this conclusion, the engineer intends to continue fishing in the river and claims to have no problem with other companies dumping chemicals.

Step 3: Make a Prediction

The engineer is not really providing any objective evidence to support the continued dumping of chemicals. Instead, the engineer's entire line of defense boils down to: "It doesn't bother me." That's the principle behind this whole argument: "If it doesn't bother me, then I can keep doing what I'm doing."

Step 4: Evaluate the Answer Choices

(C) is correct, fitting the engineer's self-centered idea that one is justified in performing an act (in this case, dumping chemicals into the river) if one is okay with accepting the consequences personally (as the engineer is willing to keep fishing and will even be fine with other companies dumping chemicals).

(A) is a Distortion. The engineer claims to be okay with other companies dumping chemicals ... if they want to. However, that's not to say that any other companies are actually planning to do so.

(B) is a 180, at worst. No benefits are mentioned. If anything, this is a reason why the engineer should stop dumping chemicals, as it could benefit those who might otherwise develop health issues.

(D) is a 180, at worst. There is evidence that the chemical dumping could impact others, and the engineer still insists on doing it. Besides, there's nothing to say whether the engineer has fully analyzed all of the possible consequences.

(E) is a 180. There's evidence that other people may be harmed, so this could provide grounds to stop dumping chemicals.

5. (B) Assumption (Necessary)

Step 1: Identify the Question Type

The question asks for an "assumption required by the ... argument," making this a Necessary Assumption question.

Step 2: Untangle the Stimulus

The strategist concludes ([c]*learly*) that, when attacking an opponent, philosophical attacks are more effective than attacks on the opponent's policies. The evidence is that philosophical attacks create a story and provide context, and that makes the attack more emotionally compelling.

Step 3: Make a Prediction

This argument has distinct Mismatched Concepts. The evidence ultimately claims that philosophical attacks are more emotionally compelling. However, does that warrant the conclusion that such attacks are more *effective*? That's not clear. For this argument to work, the author must assume that's the case, i.e., that emotionally compelling attacks are more effective.

Step 4: Evaluate the Answer Choices

(B) is correct, providing the necessary link between being emotionally compelling and being effective.

(A) is Out of Scope. It doesn't matter whether the stories are memorable or not. Even if the stories are completely forgettable, the emotional impact could still provide an effective attack.

(C) is an Irrelevant Comparison. It doesn't matter whether story-based attacks provide more or less context than other attacks. Even if story-based attacks provide relatively little context, the stories could still be emotionally compelling enough to be effective.

(D) is a Distortion. The author doesn't need policy-based attacks to be uninteresting. As long as stories are more interesting and emotionally compelling, the author's argument still stands.

(E) is a Distortion. The opponents' policy proposals don't have to be grounded to any particular overarching scheme. The strategist merely argues that the attacker should find a way to create some link to an overarching scheme, even if that scheme wasn't the opponent's basis for the proposals.

6. (B) Flaw

Step 1: Identify the Question Type
The question asks for Sam's interpretation of Michaela's remarks. It's unlikely that Sam interpreted the remarks correctly. Otherwise, that would make for a very uninteresting question. Instead, anticipate that Sam made a mistake, which would make this a Flaw question.

Step 2: Untangle the Stimulus
Michaela argues that it's unfair of doctors to complain about patients doing medical research on the Internet. She feels it's natural for people to seek being informed. Sam, on the other hand, approves of doctors complaining because they've had years of medical training. Then, Sam asks the question that comes out of nowhere: How could Michaela claim that a doctor's opinion is no better than what somebody could pull up in Google?

Step 3: Make a Prediction
That's not what Michaela said at all. Michaela just said people like to be informed. She never argued that a doctor's opinion is any less worthy. However, that was Sam's ill-informed interpretation, as the correct answer will point out.

Step 4: Evaluate the Answer Choices
(B) is correct. This paraphrases the exact claim that Sam attributes to Michaela, despite Michaela never having actually said it.

(A) is a Distortion. Sam's interpretation is about the value of such information, not how trustworthy it is. Besides, this misses the falsely implied comparison to the value of a doctor's opinion.

(C) is an Irrelevant Comparison. Sam is not questioning personal doctors versus web-published doctors. Sam is questioning doctors versus random people on the Internet.

(D) is a 180. This suggests that doctors' opinions *do* have more weight, and Sam implies that Michaela believes otherwise.

(E) is Out of Scope. There is no indication of or implication regarding people who do not research their conditions on the Internet.

7. (E) Strengthen

Step 1: Identify the Question Type
The correct answer will "help to justify" a point, making this a Strengthen question. However, read the stem carefully. The conclusion being justified is that feeding wild birds is an *exception* to the given principle. The principle will be evidence, but the correct answer will provide information why that principle does *not* apply to the given situation.

Step 2: Untangle the Stimulus
The principle is that people shouldn't feed wild animals because animals will then grow dependent on humans to survive, becoming less able to do so on their own. Yet the given situation describes how people love to feed wild birds.

Step 3: Make a Prediction
The question is, what would make birds an exception to the principle? In other words, why is it okay to feed wild birds if it's not okay to feed other wild animals? The author must assume there is something different about birds that makes feeding them okay. Don't worry about predicting a specific reason. Just look for a choice that justifies feeding birds, despite what the principle says.

Step 4: Evaluate the Answer Choices
(E) is correct. This justifies making birds an exception because we wouldn't be making birds dependent on humans; our abundant presence in their habitat alone has already made wild birds dependent on humans. Now, if we choose to follow the principle and *not* feed them, they will not survive.

(A) is a 180. Making the birds more vulnerable to predators and diseases provides even more reason to follow the principle and stop feeding the birds.

(B) is irrelevant. The principle is not about any benefit to humans. The point is that the birds are likely to suffer due to dependence on humans, and thus **(B)** does not justify ignoring the principle.

(C) is an Irrelevant Comparison. It doesn't matter where birds are more or less likely to congregate. If feeding birds makes them more dependent on humans, the principle is still valid.

(D) is Out of Scope. It doesn't matter if bird lovers are doing a lot to preserve bird habitats. If they keep feeding the birds, the birds can still become dependent on humans and the principle would still be valid. Instead—per the principle—the bird lovers should feel free to continue their preservation efforts, but stop providing the birds with food.

8. (C) Main Point

Step 1: Identify the Question Type
The question asks for the "conclusion drawn in the argument," making this a Main Point question.

Step 2: Untangle the Stimulus
The author starts by stating the usual reason political candidates send out campaign material: to influence opinions. However, the author notes that the ads Ebsen mailed out were not sent to enough people to effectively influence opinions. So, if those ads weren't trying to influence opinions, what was the point? The author has an idea. The author argues that Ebsen was merely trying to test the *potential* of those ads. To support this conclusion, the author notes how the ads covered a lot of different topics and Ebsen's campaign was spending a lot to review the results.

Step 3: Make a Prediction
The author's argument starts in at the third sentence, when the author suggests that Ebsen was merely trying to test the ads' potential. That's the conclusion. Everything before that is just context, and the last sentence is simply evidence to support the author's view about the ads.

Step 4: Evaluate the Answer Choices
(C) is correct, identifying the third sentence as the author's conclusion.

(A) is not the conclusion. This is the first sentence, but the author claims that Ebsen's ad campaign contradicts this usual process.

(B) is not the author's conclusion. As it contradicts what the first sentence describes as typical, it might feel like an author's rebuttal. However, the author provides no evidence to support this claim. There's no reason why the author believes that too few people received the ads. Thus, it's presented merely as an accepted fact, not as a conclusion.

(D) is a fact about the ads, making this a piece of evidence, not a conclusion.

(E) is a fact about the campaign, making this evidence, not a conclusion.

9. (A) Weaken

Step 1: Identify the Question Type
The question asks for something that "most weakens the argument," making this a Weaken question.

Step 2: Untangle the Stimulus
The author concludes ([*s*]*o*) that the manufacturers' increase in promotion was counterproductive, causing physicians to accept fewer visits from sales reps. The evidence is that sales reps visited an average of 640 physicians each before the promotional boost, but only 501 physicians each afterward.

Step 3: Make a Prediction
The author needs a quick refresher on how math works. The evidence is merely about a decrease in the *average* number of visits per sales rep. The conclusion suggests that the *total* number of visits went down. That assumes a relatively equal number of sales reps. If the number of sales reps went up, that could weaken the argument. After all, if the number of sales reps increased, then they could make fewer visits each while still making a greater number of visits in total. (For instance, 20 people making five one-hour visits each will make more visits in total than just 10 people making six one-hour visits each.)

Step 4: Evaluate the Answer Choices
(A) is correct. Adding more representatives can result in a larger number of visits in total (contrary to the author's claim), even if each representative doesn't make as many visits individually.

(B) is irrelevant. It doesn't matter if physicians accept the free samples or not. If the sales reps don't get to visit as many physicians, then the promotions won't work.

(C) is Out of Scope or possibly a 180. If manufacturers *had* spent the extra money on direct advertising, perhaps the promotions could have worked from a different angle. However, saying they *didn't* spend money on direct advertising, suggests they stuck to the plan of mainly visiting physicians, and the evidence implies that's not working, as the author asserts.

(D) is a 180. If physicians usually accept repeat visits and the average number of visits is dropping, that could certainly be evidence of a problem, as the author is suggesting.

(E) is a 180. If the likelihood of prescribing a drug is tied to sales visits and those visits are declining, then the author's argument is validated, not weakened.

10. (A) Main Point

Step 1: Identify the Question Type
The question asks for the "overall conclusion," making this a Main Point question.

Step 2: Untangle the Stimulus
The archaeologist starts off with an opinion, which is a good indication that this might be the conclusion. The archaeologist argues that the network of ancient tracks on Malta were probably created by erosion from wheeled vehicles. Some researchers argue otherwise, claiming that the tracks' uniform depth is evidence of manual cutting. However, the archaeologist counters their claims, suggesting that the uniformity actually indicates wheel diameter. By contradicting the researchers, this counterevidence effectively works to support the archaeologist's conclusion in the first sentence.

Step 3: Make a Prediction

The conclusion was stated at the beginning: The ancient Malta tracks were probably created by erosion from wheeled vehicles.

Step 4: Evaluate the Answer Choices

(A) correctly identifies the first sentence as the archaeologist's conclusion.

(B) is a 180. This is the researchers' view, which the archaeologist goes on to refute.

(C) is also a 180. This describes the evidence used by some researchers to support their view. However, it's just evidence, not a conclusion. Further, this is the view the archaeologist rejects.

(D) is part of the evidence at the end that the archaeologist uses to counter the research and support the conclusion. It's not the conclusion itself.

(E) is part of the counterevidence at the end. This supports the conclusion, but is not itself the conclusion.

11. (D) Paradox

Step 1: Identify the Question Type

The correct answer will "resolve the apparent discrepancy," making this a Paradox question.

Step 2: Untangle the Stimulus

According to the author, reforesting is meant to create a diverse area with multiple species of trees. *But*, some land managers reforest by planting just one type of tree.

Step 3: Make a Prediction

As with any Paradox question, it helps to paraphrase the stimulus as a question. In this case, why do some land managers plant just one type of tree if the goal is to create an area of multiple species of trees? The key to the solution likely lies in the fact that the single species used is described as "fast-growing." If the speed at which this species grows eventually makes it easier to create a more diverse forest, then that would solve the mystery.

Step 4: Evaluate the Answer Choices

(D) is correct. If trees attract wildlife, and those animals help spread a large variety of tree seeds, then that explains why managers grow the fastest tree they can. The sooner they can attract wildlife, the sooner those animals will come back and start dispersing the seeds needed to create the desired diverse forest.

(A) is irrelevant. It doesn't matter why certain trees grow faster than others. The question remains: Why plant just one species if they want a forest with multiple species?

(B) is a 180. This explains why a diverse forest is more desirable, thus making it even more mysterious why the land managers are only planting one species.

(C) does not help. This might explain why land managers don't just plant every single species they can. However, if there are multiple species that are native to the area, it would still seem worthwhile to plant all of those species and not just one of them.

(E) does not help. It might help explain why the land managers choose a species that grows quickly. However, it doesn't explain why they choose just one. If there are multiple species that grow quickly, then why not choose more than one?

12. (B) Weaken

Step 1: Identify the Question Type

The question asks for something that "seriously weakens the argument," making this a Weaken question.

Step 2: Untangle the Stimulus

The author concludes ([*o*]*bviously*) that ProBit computers are more reliable than KRV computers. The evidence is that, when looking over service requests, a computer service company found that KRV computers made up the largest proportion of requests while ProBit computers made up the smallest proportion.

Step 3: Make a Prediction

The author assumes that the proportion of service requests is indicative of reliability, i.e., the more people who contact this company to service their computers, the more unreliable those computers are. To weaken this, the correct answer should show how the number of service requests this company receives is not a trustworthy indicator of computer reliability.

Step 4: Evaluate the Answer Choices

(B) is correct, suggesting that people who need their computers serviced don't always contact the service company in question. If most people contact the manufacturer instead, it's possible that ProBit computers need a lot more servicing than the service company provides and thus may be less reliable than the author claims.

(A) is an Irrelevant Comparison. The conclusion is only about comparing ProBit to KRV. It doesn't matter how other computers fare.

(C) is a 180. If ProBit computers make up the smallest portion of this company's service requests, and that proportion is bigger than at any other company, then that suggests that other service companies are experiencing the same results: very few service requests for ProBit. That just makes the argument look even better.

(D) is irrelevant. The author claims that market share was factored in to the results, so it doesn't matter how much the computer brands differ in market share.

(E) is an Irrelevant Comparison. It doesn't matter which company has been around longer. If anything, perhaps experience helps bolster reliability, in which case this would support the author's claim of ProBit's reliability.

13. (E) Paradox
Step 1: Identify the Question Type
The correct answer will help "explain the surprising outcome," making this a Paradox question.

Step 2: Untangle the Stimulus
According to the author, scientific journals have started adding a complete online archive of articles in addition to their print archives. By doing this, scientists now have access to a lot more information and can even use a search engine to more easily find what they need. However, instead of citing a greater variety of articles, scientists are now more likely to cite the exact same articles as all the other scientists do.

Step 3: Make a Prediction
As with any Paradox question, it helps to paraphrase the mystery as a question: If scientists suddenly have access to so much more information and so many more journals, why are they all just citing the same stuff? Don't worry about predicting a specific resolution. Instead, know what the correct answer should do. In this case, it should show how all this unlimited access somehow makes it more likely for scientists to cite the same sources.

Step 4: Evaluate the Answer Choices
(E) does the trick. When using the online search tools, scientists are not looking for a variety of articles. They're looking for the articles that are already highly regarded. That just makes it more likely they're going to find the same articles that everyone else has already accepted and cited.

(A) is irrelevant. It doesn't matter which journals were available first. If many or even all of them are now available online, this still doesn't explain why the same ones are cited over and over.

(B) is Out of Scope. The scientists who *write* the articles have no bearing on this mystery. The question is why so many scientists are *citing* the same articles.

(C) does not help. Unless all scientists know each other, then this suggests that scientists should have more variety, citing different articles based on who they know. If anything, that makes it even more mysterious that everybody keeps citing the same articles.

(D) is a 180. This suggests that not only did scientists get access to all the traditional journals, but they also got access to several *new* journals. That should have led to more diversity, not less.

14. (C) Strengthen
Step 1: Identify the Question Type
The question asks for something that *strengthens* the argument, making this a Strengthen question.

Step 2: Untangle the Stimulus
According to the research, people have the ability to look at a neutral picture of someone else and determine whether or not that person is extroverted. The same ability can be used to determine dominance when looking at neutral pictures of chimps. As humans and chimps are both primates, the researcher concludes that this ability is acquired biologically and not culturally.

Step 3: Make a Prediction
It's reasonable to believe that humans and chimps constitute different cultures, so it's reasonable to argue that this ability is not culturally acquired. But does that mean it has to be biological? The author assumes so. To strengthen this argument, the author should show how the recognized traits (extroversion and dominance) are somehow connected to primate biology.

Step 4: Evaluate the Answer Choices
(C) is correct, showing how extroversion and dominance are biologically related, i.e., they're both part of one's genetics regarding assertiveness.

(A) is a 180, at worst. If this ability doesn't work on bonobos (which are primates), then maybe it's not a primate thing after all.

(B) is an Irrelevant Comparison. The argument is not about which traits or how many can be identified. It's about *how* we're able to identify them, and this offers no support for the biological theory.

(D) is Out of Scope. The history of primate ancestry has nothing to do with what creates our ability to recognize certain traits.

(E) is Out of Scope. It doesn't matter who specifically is in the photos. The argument is about how we recognize extroversion or dominance, regardless of whose face is in the picture.

15. (E) Flaw
Step 1: Identify the Question Type
The question asks why the argument is "vulnerable to criticism," which is common wording for a Flaw question.

Step 2: Untangle the Stimulus
The author concludes ([*t*]*herefore*) that most old houses on 20th Avenue have multiple apartments. The evidence is that there are twice as many apartments as there are old houses, and only old houses have apartments.

Step 3: Make a Prediction
The math works well if the apartments are evenly spread out. For example, if there were 10 old houses and 20 apartments, even distribution would put 2 apartments per old house, confirming the author's conclusion. However, what if 8 of the houses had just a single apartment each, while the remaining 2 offered 6 apartments each? In that case—there'd still be 10 old houses and 20 apartments—but most of the houses would have just 1 apartment, contradicting the author's conclusion. So, the flaw is that the author assumes a relatively even distribution. Any answer that questions the distribution of apartments to old houses will reveal that flaw.

Step 4: Evaluate the Answer Choices
(E) is correct. If a lot of old houses have 3, 4, or even 10 apartments, then most of the apartments could be clustered in just a few old houses, leaving most old houses with just 1, if any, apartments.

(A) is irrelevant. The argument is only about old houses, and the first sentence mentions that all apartments are in old houses. So, even if new houses (or other types of buildings) exist, they don't matter. They don't have apartments, and thus they don't factor into this argument.

(B) is inaccurate. The conclusion is about the number of houses with multiple apartments, a statistic that is distinct from the evidence (which only provides the number of houses overall versus the number of apartments overall).

(C) is irrelevant. The argument is only about apartments, so other types of rental accommodations don't matter.

(D) describes the commonly tested flaw of confusing sufficiency and necessity. However, nothing is said to be sufficient for claiming that houses have multiple apartments, and nothing is implied to be necessary for making such a claim.

16. (A) Weaken

Step 1: Identify the Question Type
The question asks for something that *weakens* the given argument, making this a Weaken question.

Step 2: Untangle the Stimulus
According to the scientist, the atmosphere around Venus experienced a short spike in sulfur dioxide. Volcanoes cause that to happen on Earth, and Venus has lots of mountains that were previously volcanic. *But*, the scientist argues that volcanic activity did *not* cause the spike around Venus. The evidence is that no active volcanoes have been found on Venus yet, and atmospheric changes are sometimes just part of a cycle.

Step 3: Make a Prediction
While volcanoes offer a possible explanation for the spike in sulfur dioxide, the scientist offers a plausible alternative: It

could just have been part of a cyclical variation. However, are volcanoes really ruled out? The only evidence is that an active volcano hasn't been discovered yet. That doesn't mean they don't exist. To weaken this argument, it can be shown that volcanoes might actually exist and/or that they could be responsible for the sulfur dioxide spike, contrary to the scientist's claims.

Step 4: Evaluate the Answer Choices
(A) is correct. If conditions on Venus make it difficult to spot volcanic activity directly, that would explain why active volcanoes haven't been identified. In that case, a volcano could have erupted without notice and caused the spike in sulfur dioxide, contrary to what the scientist argues.

(B) is irrelevant. What caused that spike 30 years ago? Is that the timing of the cycle, that sulfur dioxide rises quickly every 30 years? Did a volcano erupt back then? This does nothing to either support or deny the scientist's claims.

(C) is an Irrelevant Comparison. It doesn't matter which atmosphere has more sulfur dioxide. The argument is about where that sulfur dioxide comes from.

(D) is irrelevant. It doesn't matter how long the sulfur dioxide lingers. This does nothing to confirm or deny whether the sulfur dioxide around Venus came from a volcano.

(E) is irrelevant, and a 180 at worst. The argument is about the source of sulfur dioxide around Venus, not Earth. Besides, this indicates that volcanoes are not the only source of sulfur dioxide spikes. That suggests there could be alternative explanations for the spike around Venus, strengthening the scientist's claim that volcanoes may not have been the cause.

17. (C) Inference

Step 1: Identify the Question Type
The correct answer will be "strongly supported by the information" in the stimulus, making this an Inference question.

Step 2: Untangle the Stimulus
The stimulus provides a lot of statistics about transmission lines. When their electric load increases, their temperature rises. Too much load can make the lines too hot to operate. However, wind can help cool the temperature. Additionally, it's noted that stronger winds cool more than light winds, and cross breezes cool more than parallel breezes.

Step 3: Make a Prediction
There are too many possible inferences to predict here. However, consider the implication of the last few lines. According to the beginning, too much load can cause lines to overheat. However, if winds can help cool the lines down, that could prevent the lines from overheating, allowing them to handle more load than if the wind was absent. The correct answer is likely to use this implication.

Step 4: Evaluate the Answer Choices

(C) is supported. When winds are stronger, they cool the lines more, suggesting that the lines can now handle more load than previously.

(A) is Out of Scope. While windy days would allow the lines to handle a higher load, there's no evidence to suggest that utility companies take advantage of that and actually increase the load.

(B) is a 180. Lines parallel to the wind are not cooled as much as those perpendicular to the wind, and thus parallel lines are likely to overheat faster. They would thus be able to carry *smaller* loads, not greater loads.

(D) is an Irrelevant Comparision. The author provides no information about how air temperature affects transmission lines.

(E) is a Distortion. On windy days, the lines can be kept cooler and perhaps handle more loads. However, that doesn't change the maximum operating temperature. Once the line hits a given temperature, it stops working.

18. (A) Strengthen

Step 1: Identify the Question Type
The question asks for something that "most supports" the given hypothesis, making this a Strengthen question.

Step 2: Untangle the Stimulus
The author is discussing "fairy circles"—large, vegetation-free patches of ground found in grasslands near the Namib Desert. The hypothesis is that burrowing sand termites are responsible for these patches. The evidence is that sand termites were found in every such circular patch.

Step 3: Make a Prediction
This argument is a perfect example of the flaw of correlation versus causation. Sand termites were found in every such patch where the grass stopped growing, but are they really responsible for those patches? The author fails to consider other possible causes. Also, the author places the cause specifically on the burrowing activity. How does burrowing affect vegetation growth? The author provides no evidence. Any choice that provides further evidence that termites and/or their burrowing plays a role in clearing out the vegetation will strengthen the argument.

Step 4: Evaluate the Answer Choices
(A) is correct. If the damage only occurs at the roots, that eliminates alternative above-ground causes and makes it more likely that something is happening underground—such as burrowing.

(B) is irrelevant. This does nothing to support that termites had any role in the clearing of those patches. Besides, this only describes the grass surrounding those patches. It

doesn't necessarily give any indication of what happened to the grass that used to be in those patches.

(C) is a 180, at worst. This suggests a significant way in which the soil in the patches differ from the surrounding land. If there's more water, it could be too much to support vegetation, and that could be the real issue, not the termites.

(D) is irrelevant. This suggests that, once many circles form, others are likely to follow. However, it does nothing to support what causes them in the first place.

(E) is irrelevant. If anything, this suggests that some predators know how to find a home near a good food source. However, this does nothing to confirm that the termites are responsible for ridding that area of vegetation.

19. (B) Parallel Reasoning

Step 1: Identify the Question Type
The correct answer will be an argument that is "parallel in its reasoning" to the argument in the stimulus. That makes this a Parallel Reasoning question.

Step 2: Untangle the Stimulus
It is given that Munroe won the election. The author then provides some Formal Logic. To have won, Munroe needed a shift in the electorate's sentiments and a well-run campaign. *Thus*, the author concludes that the electorate's sentiments shifted.

Step 3: Make a Prediction
The Formal Logic will be important here. It provides two requirements for an event to happen. In this case, winning the election required shifting sentiments and a well-run campaign.

If	**Munroe wins**	→	**shift in sentiment AND well-run campaign**

In addition, it's given that the event happened (i.e., Munroe won). Thus, it can be concluded that both requirements were met. Yet, the author oddly chose to conclude about only one of those requirements, which is still a valid conclusion. In any event, the correct answer should provide the same structure: Two requirements are presented for an event to occur, and the author concludes that one of those requirements was met because the event did occur. Algebraically, the argument is If X, then Y and Z. Therefore, since X, must have Y.

Step 4: Evaluate the Answer Choices
(B) is correct. The author provides two requirements for an event to occur (the cafe closing (X) was dependent on strong competition (Y) and unsatisfied customers (Z).

| If | Park Street Cafe closes | → | facing strong competition AND customer base unsatisfied |

The cafe did close, and the author concludes that one of the requirements (strong competition) was met.

(A) does not match. There's no Formal Logic providing necessary conditions. Furthermore, unlike the original argument, there's no evidence to support the conclusion, i.e., no reason why the author even brings up competition (for the first time) in the conclusion.

(C) does not match. There's no Formal Logic providing two necessary conditions. Instead, the author concludes that one reason is unjustified (you can't say the customers were unsatisfied) because another reason had to be true (there must have been competition).

(D) does not match. The Formal Logic provides two sufficient conditions instead of two necessary conditions. Further, the author concludes that both conditions might have been met, not just one.

(E) does not match. The Formal Logic does provide two necessary conditions: To stay open, the cafe needed no competition and happy customers.

| If | Park Street Cafe open | → | ~ competition AND satisfied customer base |

However, unlike the original, the sufficient term did *not* occur—the cafe did not stay open—whereas, in the stimulus, Munroe *did* win the election. In **(E)**, evidence is given that both requirements went unsatisfied. The author then concludes that the event couldn't possibly have occurred.

| If | competition OR ~ satisfied customer based | → | Park Street Cafe ~ open |

That's a completely different argument that's predicated on forming the contrapositive of the original statement.

20. (B) Inference

Step 1: Identify the Question Type
The correct answer will be "strongly supported by" the stimulus, making this an Inference question.

Step 2: Untangle the Stimulus
According to the author, bumblebees are more efficient than honeybees at pollinating certain crops (e.g., cranberries). Why? Because bumblebees stick to a small area and visit just a few species of plants, while honeybees will go anywhere and visit a lot more species.

Step 3: Make a Prediction
The implication here is that pollinating efficiency (particularly for cranberries and similar crops) is affected by how far bees will travel and how many other plants they'll visit. For cranberries and similar crops, it's more efficient for the bees to stay close and only visit a few other plants (as bumblebees do).

Step 4: Evaluate the Answer Choices
(B) is correct. The author directly says that bumblebees are more efficient *because* they only visit a few plants, as opposed to those honeybees, who will visit just about any plant that says hello.

(A) is Extreme. The visiting habits of the honeybee are only said to make it less efficient for pollinating "certain crops," not *any* crop it visits.

(C) is a 180, at worst. If anything, the opposite is suggested as the honeybee covers a broader area and visits more, not fewer, species.

(D) is a Distortion. It's not that honeybees are less likely to visit cranberries. It's just that honeybees are more likely to travel further and visit other plants in addition to the cranberries, while the bumblebees tend to cover a smaller area.

(E) is not supported. Even if a certain honeybee is guaranteed to visit one or more plants in a cranberry crop (maybe it lives immediately next to it), that doesn't make it more efficient at pollinating that crop, because that honeybee will also travel over a broad area and pollinate many other species. Conversely, a certain bumblebee may be likely but not certain to visit a specific cranberry crop (it lives a small distance away), but if it does visit that crop it would still be more efficient than the honeybee. Nothing in the stimulus supports a proportional relationship between likelihood of visiting a specific crop and efficiency in pollinating that crop.

21. (A) Assumption (Sufficient)

Step 1: Identify the Question Type
The correct answer, "if ... assumed," will logically complete the argument. That makes this a Sufficient Assumption question.

Step 2: Untangle the Stimulus
The economist concludes ([s]o) that banks are lending less to companies than they did five years ago. The evidence is that they're lending less to small and medium-sized companies,

and they won't lend to companies that aren't financially strong. As for large, financially strong companies, they would pay the banks lower interest rates than the banks would pay to borrow that money.

Step 3: Make a Prediction

The conclusion is about the total amount of lending being done. By the evidence, less is definitely being lent to small and medium businesses, and businesses that are not financially strong are getting nothing. That leaves one more piece of the puzzle: large businesses that *are* financially strong. If banks are not lending as much to them, then total lending is definitely down. However, the economist never actually says that banks aren't lending as much to large businesses. The economist only says that those businesses would pay lower interest rates than the banks pay. That doesn't mean the banks aren't loaning them money. However, if the author assumes that banks *do* refuse to loan those companies money, then everything is settled: Total lending is definitely down.

Step 4: Evaluate the Answer Choices

(A) is correct. If banks won't lend money at rates lower than the ones they themselves pay, then they won't lend to large businesses. Additionally, they're loaning less to small and medium businesses. That accounts for everything, guaranteeing the conclusion that total lending is down.

(B) is irrelevant. It doesn't matter if small and medium companies are financially strong. They're already being lent less, so that's accounted for. It's the large businesses that still aren't accounted for.

(C) is not good enough. This would certainly help, as companies that are not financially strong now get nothing. However, there's still the open-ended issue of large companies that *are* financially strong. They could still be getting more loans, so **(C)** does not guarantee the conclusion.

(D) is irrelevant. Even if the banks are now paying higher interest rates, it's still not known whether banks are lending money to large businesses or not. The argument is still incomplete.

(E) is an Irrelevant Comparison. The argument is not about who gets a better interest rate. The argument relies solely on knowing whether businesses are getting loans or not.

22. (B) Inference

Step 1: Identify the Question Type

The correct answer "must be false" based on the given statements. That makes this an Inference question. Even though such questions don't usually ask for a false statement, the question requires taking the given information and using it as evidence to support choosing the correct answer. That's how Inference questions work.

Step 2: Untangle the Stimulus

The stimulus consists of a lot of Formal Logic. The first claim provides a necessary condition for being kind to someone: You need to want that person to prosper.

If	*kind*	→	***want other to prosper***

The second claim is not conditional, instead just noting that two people can dislike each other and *may* still be respectful to each other. The last two claims, though, are both conditional. First, if two people dislike each other, they cannot be content in each other's presence.

If	*dislike*	→	*~ content*

Finally, if two people do *not* dislike each other, they will be kind to each other.

If	*~ dislike*	→	*kind*

Step 3: Make a Prediction

First things first: Throw out the second sentence. In a question that asks for something that *must* be false, the second sentence is useless. It claims that people who dislike each other *may* respect each other. But maybe they won't. Who knows? It can't be determined for sure, so it will never be absolutely true or absolutely false.

As for the rest, start with the contrapositive of the claim about being content. By contrapositive of the previous logic, if two people *are* content in each other's presence, then they can't dislike each other.

If	*content*	→	*~ dislike*

With that, all of the Formal Logic statements can be combined to form a complete string. If two people are content, they don't dislike each other, which (by the last sentence) means they will be kind to each other, which in turn (by the first sentence) means they want each other to prosper.

If	*content*	→	*~ dislike*	→	*kind*	→	***want other to prosper***

For a statement to be false, it will present any sufficient condition and suggest that the necessary result does not happen.

Step 4: Evaluate the Answer Choices

(B) is correct. According to the logic, if two people are content, they don't dislike each other, which means they're kind, which means they *must* want each other to prosper. It is impossible (i.e., must be false) for them to *not* want each other to prosper.

(A) is a Distortion. If two people are content, then they don't dislike each other (i.e., they might like each other). However, that doesn't mean if they *do* like each other that they must be content in each other's presence. That would require improperly reversing the logic. It's still possible, as this choice claims, that they are not content in each other's presence.

(C) could still be true. The claim about respect only says *may*. If two people treat each other with respect, they may dislike each other ... or they may not. Without knowing for sure, it's impossible to know whether or not they are content in each other's presence.

(D) is a Distortion. Wanting each other to prosper is the final necessary condition of the chain and thus does not allow for any absolute deductions. If two people want each other to prosper, they may or may not be kind to each other, which means they may or may not dislike each other. It could go either way.

(E) could still be true. People who are kind to each other must want each other to succeed. However, there is no evidence linking either of those concepts to respect. Moreover, even if there was, the only claim about respect here uses *may*, so it would be impossible to conclude that this is absolutely false.

23. (C) Parallel Flaw

Step 1: Identify the Question Type
The question asks for "flawed reasoning" that is "most similar" to that found in the stimulus. That makes this a Parallel Flaw question. However, the question does not say *the* flawed reasoning, which means there may not be just one flaw. There may be multiple flaws, and the correct answer can reproduce just one of those flaws and ignore the others.

Step 2: Untangle the Stimulus
The author concludes ([*t*]*hus*) that people who regularly drink soft drinks with aspartame will develop a preference for really sweet stuff. The evidence is that aspartame is sweeter than sugar, so (the author argues) soft drinks with aspartame must be sweeter than those with sugar.

Step 3: Make a Prediction
Does regular consumption of soda with aspartame really cause people to suddenly crave a lot of sweets? That seems a stretch. Soda is only one part of a person's diet, and there's no evidence that people's enjoyment of one sweet product will suddenly make them prefer everything to be particularly sweet. The correct answer could commit the same error:

claiming that, just because people prefer one item with a certain trait, they will develop an overall preference of other items to have that certain trait.

However, that is not parallel to any of the choices. So, there must be another flaw being tested. There's one in drawing the subsidiary conclusion. The author argues that soft drinks with aspartame are sweeter than those with sugar, because aspartame is sweeter than sugar ... in equal quantities (one gram). However, what if soft drinks with aspartame use a lot less aspartame? That could reduce the sweetness, meaning they need not taste a lot sweeter than the soft drinks with sugar. So, if a correct answer contains that same flaw (assuming two items of different degree appear in equal quantities), it will be correct.

Step 4: Evaluate the Answer Choices

(C) is correct. Yes, one nickel is worth more than one penny. However, if Joe's bank has a lot fewer nickels than Maria's bank has pennies, then Joe need not have more money overall. It's the same mistake the original argument makes in suggesting that aspartame-filled sodas must be sweeter overall.

(A) does not match. This choice could tempt people who focused on the parallel content (food preferences) rather than on the parallel logic. However, this argument takes a possible outcome (people *sometimes* develop a preference) and concludes it will certainly happen (it will *eventually* occur). That's a flaw, but not one committed in the original argument.

(B) does not match. This states that items are not found in equal quantity, so it cannot match the original argument, which assumes that items *are* in equal quantity. While this argument may be flawed (for one, it assumes people read the books they own), that flaw is not one committed in the original argument.

(D) does not match. This reverses the logic of the original argument. Here, the evidence is that one person has a preference for something (Stephanie likes hot weather) and the conclusion is that the person had more exposure to that (Stephanie grew up with more hot weather). In the original, exposure (drinking more sweet soda) was the evidence, and developing a preference was the conclusion. They are different arguments with different flaws.

(E) does not match. The logic is flawed in assuming that Guillermo and Abdul will use their personal experience as a basis for their estimates. However, there is no flaw in the original argument about assuming the use of personal experience.

24. (A) Strengthen

Step 1: Identify the Question Type
The question asks for something that "most strengthens" the argument, making this a Strengthen question.

Step 2: Untangle the Stimulus
The economist's argument is based on evaluating the pros and cons of increasing the minimum wage. If the minimum wage is not increased, employers will be willing to hire more people, but they won't invest in technology to boost productivity. On the other hand, if the minimum wage *is* increased, productivity would increase, although employers would start cutting back on hiring. From this, the economist concludes ([*t*]*hus*) that raising the minimum wage would be overall better for the economy.

Step 3: Make a Prediction
The entire argument boils down to jobs versus productivity. By supporting the higher minimum wage, the economist is putting a premium on productivity. To strengthen this argument, the correct answer should provide more evidence in favor of promoting productivity.

Step 4: Evaluate the Answer Choices
(A) is correct. This suggests a fantastic benefit to productivity: It can create new jobs. In that case, increasing productivity can eventually help minimize the job issue, making it a winning proposition.

(B) is a 180. If unemployment is already a growing problem, that makes raising the minimum wage, which would cut back on hiring, look like a worse plan, not a better one.

(C) is a 180. If unemployment is a key factor, then a higher minimum wage, which would reduce hiring, does not look like a good idea.

(D) is an Irrelevant Comparison. The argument does not address the *development* of new technology. The question is whether employers would be willing to *buy* new technology, regardless of who's developing it. Plus, it's only productivity-enhancing technology that's of interest, not technology in general.

(E) is a 180. If such technology gets old fast, then it seems less warranted to support the plan that would encourage buying more such technology.

25. (D) Role of a Statement

Step 1: Identify the Question Type
The question provides a claim from the stimulus and asks for the *role* that claim plays in the argument. That makes this a Role of a Statement question.

Step 2: Untangle the Stimulus
The mayor starts with a story about ice cream. You know how some ice cream companies occasionally offer free ice cream? It sounds great, but you're sacrificing a lot of time (too many people, long lines) just to save a few bucks. In short, giving away something valuable for free is a bad idea. The mayor then applies this same logic to rush-hour traffic, which is lots of people stuck in long lines. The mayor's solution? Stop making it free. Charge people to drive during rush hour.

Step 3: Make a Prediction
Terrible analogy aside, the mayor's conclusion is the recommendation to charge people for driving during rush hour. The claim in question is the third sentence about getting overconsumption and long lines when you offer something for free. That's the general principle underlying the mayor's ice cream parable. The author then uses that principle to support the recommendation of charging rush-hour fees. So, the correct answer will describe how the claim in question is a principle used to support the author's conclusion.

Step 4: Evaluate the Answer Choices
(D) is correct.

(A) is a 180. The author does not reject the claim in question. The author accepts it and uses it to support a recommendation.

(B) is a Distortion. The analogy is certainly disputable, but such dispute is never mentioned or addressed in the argument.

(C) is a 180. It *is* used as evidence to support the conclusion. Why is a system needed to charge people that use roads during rush hour? Because "when something valuable costs no money you get overconsumption and long lines."

(E) is inaccurate. The conclusion is the author's recommendation to charge fees for rush-hour driving.

26. (D) Strengthen

Step 1: Identify the Question Type
The question asks for something that "adds the most support" for the argument, making this a Strengthen question.

Step 2: Untangle the Stimulus
The author notes how an auto insurance company has a wide variety of ads, from offbeat to informative. While most companies use one type of ad in order to establish an identity among their target audience, the author concludes that variety is better for auto insurance companies. The evidence is that auto insurance consumers are demographically diverse.

Step 3: Make a Prediction
The argument relies on Mismatched Concepts, assuming that variety is better for companies with a diverse demographic. Any answer that validates that assumption will strengthen the argument.

Step 4: Evaluate the Answer Choices

(D) is correct. If targeting just one audience would alienate others, then that supports why variety would be good for auto insurance companies, which need to attract a diverse set of audiences.

(A) is a 180. If single-audience ads can appeal to a wider audience than expected, then that offers no reason why the auto insurance companies would need to create a variety of ads.

(B) is a 180. According to the author, brand identity is created by a uniform set of ads, not a variety of ads. If brand identity is critical, then this goes against the author's argument that variety is good.

(C) is an Irrelevant Comparison, and a 180 at worst. If fewer people are influenced by the insurance ads, then that may suggest the variety isn't working very well, contrary to the author's claim.

(E) is Out of Scope. Although some ads may miss the mark, there's no evidence that any of Roadwise's ads "fall short." So, **(E)** does not provide a justification for why variety is a "smart approach." Furthermore, companies that use a uniform approach and those that use a variety seek to "influence a target demographic." So, the fact that ads can fail does not clearly benefit either strategy.

Section III: Logical Reasoning

Q#	Question Type	Correct	Difficulty
1	Inference	B	★
2	Strengthen/Weaken (Evaluate the Argument)	A	★
3	Point at Issue	B	★
4	Assumption (Sufficient)	B	★
5	Inference	D	★
6	Principle (Identify/Strengthen)	A	★★
7	Flaw	E	★
8	Paradox	A	★
9	Flaw	C	★★
10	Principle (Identify/Strengthen)	C	★★
11	Parallel Flaw	C	★
12	Assumption (Sufficient)	B	★
13	Flaw	A	★
14	Inference	D	★
15	Method of Argument	C	★★
16	Inference	E	★★★★
17	Assumption (Necessary)	C	★★
18	Flaw	E	★★★
19	Assumption (Necessary)	E	★★★
20	Weaken	D	★★★
21	Assumption (Necessary)	E	★★★★
22	Weaken	E	★★★★
23	Paradox	A	★
24	Flaw	B	★★★★
25	Parallel Reasoning	C	★★

1. (B) Inference

Step 1: Identify the Question Type
For this question, the given statements will be used to "strongly support" the correct answer, making this an Inference question.

Step 2: Untangle the Stimulus
The author describes a research experiment in which two electrodes were placed in a dolphin's pool. When the electrodes were off, the dolphin swam as normal. However, when the electrodes were activated, the dolphin swam away. The researchers then put plastic over certain organs (vibrissal crypts) on the dolphin's nose. With the plastic cover, dolphins no longer swam away from activated electrodes.

Step 3: Make a Prediction
The first half of the experiment suggests that the dolphin was somehow disturbed by the electric field created by the electrodes. However, when the vibrissal crypts were covered, the dolphin was no longer disturbed by the electric field. This supports, as the correct answer should say, that those snout organs are what the electric fields affect.

Step 4: Evaluate the Answer Choices
(B) is correct, making the implied link between the vibrissal crypts and the electric fields.

(A) is Out of Scope. The research only indicates how the dolphin behaves, not what one would or wouldn't encounter in the wild.

(C) is a 180 and Distortion. In the first half of the experiment, the dolphin *did* instinctively avoid the electric fields. Also, the dolphin wasn't trained to avoid them. The dolphin's sensory organs were covered in plastic.

(D) is a Distortion. There's nothing to suggest that the vibrissal crypts were functioning abnormally. Perhaps those crypts were supposed to warn the dolphin of electric fields, and they were acting normally until they were covered.

(E) is a 180. The dolphin seemed to sense the electric fields just fine until its snout was covered.

2. (A) Strengthen/Weaken (Evaluate the Argument)

Step 1: Identify the Question Type
The correct answer will be a question that would "help in evaluating" the given argument. That makes this an Evaluate the Argument question, which is a variation of Strengthen/Weaken questions. To evaluate an argument, a question should address the assumption in a way that, depending on how that question is answered, would deem the argument more valid or less.

Step 2: Untangle the Stimulus
As part of a study, customers paying cash at certain retail stores were given an extra dollar with their change. The author concludes ([s]o) that most of these people were being dishonest. The evidence is that most people didn't return the extra dollar.

Step 3: Make a Prediction
Is keeping the extra dollar really a sign of dishonesty? Dishonesty implies that people were intentionally lying or withholding the truth, but the author overlooks another possibility. What if they honestly didn't know they were given an extra dollar? The author assumes they knew and just didn't say anything. The correct answer will question the validity of this assumption.

Step 4: Evaluate the Answer Choices
(A) is correct. If people were counting their change, then they were more likely to realize the error, strengthening the claim that they were dishonestly keeping the money. However, if people were not counting the change, then they wouldn't have known they received an extra dollar. Thus, it's not dishonesty; it's just not paying attention.

(B) is irrelevant. The argument is only about those who paid cash, so it doesn't matter how many such people were involved or their proportion with respect to those who used other transaction types.

(C) is irrelevant. The argument is not concerned about how people would describe themselves. The honest/dishonest label is given by the author; it's immaterial how people would label themselves. Furthermore, the conclusion is about those that *didn't* return the dollar, not those who did.

(D) is irrelevant. It doesn't matter what was going through the minds of those who *did* return the dollar. It's the people who *didn't* return the dollar with whom the author is concerned.

(E) is irrelevant. The conclusion is about how people behaved in this circumstance, not how they would behave in other circumstances involving more money.

3. (B) Point at Issue

Step 1: Identify the Question Type
The stimulus provides two speakers and the question asks for something those speakers "disagree over," making this a Point at Issue question.

Step 2: Untangle the Stimulus
Dario argues that all new drug compounds should receive patents because patents reward the research involved and promote further innovation. Cynthia agrees about the value of innovation, but uses that to argue that only truly innovative drugs, not minor variants, should receive patents. Minor variants are cheaper to create and companies like to focus on cheap.

Step 3: Make a Prediction
Dario and Cynthia actually agree on a number of points, but the ultimate point at issue comes down to what drugs should be patented. Dario argues they should all be patented, but

Cynthia argues that patents should only be given to certain drugs—those that are truly innovative. The correct answer will address this contention about which drugs deserve patents.

Step 4: Evaluate the Answer Choices

(B) is correct. Dario makes this claim and would thus agree with it. Cynthia argues there should be exceptions (no minor variants) and would thus disagree with this claim. Those opinions are contrary to each other, confirming this as the point at issue.

(A) is a 180. Dario and Cynthia both claim that innovation is important. They would agree about this.

(C) is a 180. They would agree that developing such drugs is expensive. Dario calls all drug development costly, and Cynthia claims that developing truly innovative drugs is more expensive than merely tweaking existing ones.

(D) is Out of Scope for Dario. Dario does not address any incentive to creating minor variants, and thus would have no expressed reason to dispute such a claim by Cynthia.

(E) is a 180. Both speakers would agree that patents *can* promote innovation. Dario directly makes that claim, and Cynthia agrees that patents can promote innovation, as long as they're limited to the truly innovative drugs.

4. (B) Assumption (Sufficient)

Step 1: Identify the Question Type

The correct answer will allow the conclusion to be drawn, "if [it] is assumed," making this a Sufficient Assumption question.

Step 2: Untangle the Stimulus

According to the author, there are only two reasons why it would be wrong to perform certain pollution-causing actions: 1) Pollution harms ecosystems, and 2) pollution harms people. Despite that, the author concludes that it's okay to perform mining operations on Mars, even though it would create pollution. The evidence is that any people there wouldn't be harmed.

Step 3: Make a Prediction

Okay, so the pollution won't harm people. However, the author said there were *two* reasons to avoid polluting. What about the ecosystem of Mars? If the ecosystem there is harmed, that would be a reason to stop mining. The author is assuming that won't happen, i.e., that no ecosystem on Mars will be harmed by the pollution.

Step 4: Evaluate the Answer Choices

(B) is correct, perhaps in a way that is stronger than anticipated. If there are no ecosystems at all, then no ecosystem can be harmed. That more than sufficiently provides the missing link.

(A) is an Irrelevant Comparison. It's not about what actions pollute more than others. If mining harms the ecosystem at all, then it shouldn't be done.

(C) is Out of Scope. Economic benefits do not play any role in this argument.

(D) is Out of Scope. The argument is about whether or not mining *should* be done, not whether or not it *can* be.

(E) is a Distortion. This refers to the author's point that ecosystems are valuable. However, determining the value of an ecosystem provides no evidence that any such ecosystem on Mars is being harmed.

5. (D) Inference

Step 1: Identify the Question Type

The correct answer will fill in the blank at the end of the argument. As the blank is preceded by [*t*]*hus*, that blank will contain a claim supported by everything else in the stimulus. That makes this an Inference question.

Step 2: Untangle the Stimulus

The author provides two statistics about people with low self-esteem: 1) They're treated disrespectfully more often than people with high self-esteem, and 2) they're more likely to feel disrespected even when they receive the same treatment as people with high self-esteem.

Step 3: Make a Prediction

So, what does all this say about people with low self-esteem? Well, they're more likely to be disrespected. Moreover, even if they are treated with respect, if they're treated the same as everyone else, they're still likely to *feel* disrespected. In short, the author is implying that people with low self-esteem are destined to feel more disrespected, no matter what.

Step 4: Evaluate the Answer Choices

(D) is correct, summarizing the author's view that people with low self-esteem are going to feel disrespected more than other people.

(A) is a Distortion. Even if they're treated with respect like everyone else, people with low self-esteem can feel disrespected, and they're likely to feel disrespected when they actually are disrespected. However, it's not given which situation happens more often, so it can't be said if they're usually right or wrong.

(B) is a Distortion. While the author does imply a connection between respect and self-esteem, it's not necessarily a causal connection. And even if it is, the reverse is equally likely: It could be that low self-esteem is the cause of people being disrespected.

(C) is Out of Scope. The author does not suggest why people with low self-esteem are more often disrespected. It may be because others notice their low self-esteem, but it could be for countless other reasons.

(E) is also Out of Scope. The author only provides information on how people are treated, not how they treat others.

6. (A) Principle (Identify/Strengthen)

Step 1: Identify the Question Type
The question directly asks for a principle, making this an Identify the Principle question. Furthermore, the principle will be used to "strongly support" a conclusion, which means this will also work like a Strengthen question.

Step 2: Untangle the Stimulus
Watanabe argues that, to protect kokanee salmon, trout fishing should be permitted because trout eat a lot of kokanee. Lopez argues that there's a better solution. Instead of allowing trout fishing, focus on getting rid of mysis shrimp. Those shrimp were added to the lake as food for the kokanee, but the shrimp wound up eating plankton, which is what young kokanee eat.

Step 3: Make a Prediction
Lopez's conclusion is that targeting the shrimp is better than targeting the trout. To justify that conclusion, a principle would have to provide a basis for choosing the shrimp plan over the trout plan, based on the details Lopez provides.

Step 4: Evaluate the Answer Choices
(A) is correct. The trout are said to be native while the shrimp are introduced (i.e., non-native). If it's better to eliminate non-native species, then that justifies Lopez's suggestion.

(B) is Out of Scope. There is no evidence for which plan would produce the quicker results, so this couldn't help justify one plan over the other.

(C) is a 180. This would weaken Lopez's plan, which calls for eliminating a species (the mysis shrimp) from the area.

(D) is Out of Scope. The non-native species (mysis shrimp) has already been introduced. Lopez's plan is to get rid of that species, not prevent new ones from being added.

(E) is Out of Scope and a possible 180. Lopez and Watanabe are only concerned with protecting the kokanee salmon, not increasing its population. Even so, if increasing the population is needed to get back to standard levels, this principle runs counter to Lopez's recommendation. Eliminating shrimp hurts the mature salmon in their prime, which eat the shrimp; eliminating shrimp helps the young salmon because the shrimp will no longer eat the food source of the young salmon.

7. (E) Flaw

Step 1: Identify the Question Type
The correct answer will describe why the argument is "vulnerable to criticism," which makes this a Flaw question.

Step 2: Untangle the Stimulus
The author concludes that rational-choice theory cannot be correct. The evidence is that rational-choice theory claims people only act when they expect it will benefit them, but there are plenty of examples of people acting and not receiving any benefit.

Step 3: Make a Prediction
The author makes a small but significant shift in scope. According to the theory, people will act only if they *expect* a benefit. The supposed counterevidence only shows how some people didn't *actually* benefit. That doesn't mean they weren't expecting one. They may have still expected a benefit but just failed to receive one. The author doesn't consider that, and the correct answer will point out this overlooked possibility.

Step 4: Evaluate the Answer Choices
(E) is correct, pointing out the overlooked possibility that people may have still expected a benefit even if they didn't get one.

(A) describes circular reasoning, but the author provides distinct evidence to support the conclusion. The evidence is inadequate, but it's not redundant.

(B) is a Distortion. The author does not mention evidence in favor of the theory. The author only provides evidence against that theory, and that evidence is actual evidence not hypothetical.

(C) is a Distortion. The author rejects the theory based on people who did *not* actually benefit. People who do actually benefit are not relevant.

(D) is an Irrelevant Comparison. The author's argument rests solely on the mere existence of examples of people not benefiting. It doesn't matter if such examples are more or less common than ones in which people do benefit.

8. (A) Paradox

Step 1: Identify the Question Type
The question asks for something that "helps to explain" a situation, making this a Paradox question.

Step 2: Untangle the Stimulus
According to the author, wind is created by differences in atmospheric temperature. However, Jupiter has stronger winds than Earth, even though the Sun is too far away to affect Jupiter's atmosphere as it does Earth's atmosphere.

Step 3: Make a Prediction
Paraphrase the mystery as a question: Why does Jupiter have such strong winds if the Sun is too far away to impact its atmosphere? The problem is that the first sentence says that wind is created by temperature differences, not just the Sun. While the Sun affects temperatures around the Earth, perhaps Jupiter has another heat source that affects temperatures

even more, thus producing stronger winds. The correct answer will likely describe such an alternate heat source.

Step 4: Evaluate the Answer Choices

(A) is correct, providing an alternate source of wind-impacting heat for Jupiter: the planet's own internal heat source. That could also explain why Jupiter's winds are so much stronger. The temperatures are affected by a heat source within the planet itself. Earth's temperatures are affected by the Sun, which is millions of miles away. (About 93 million, if we want to get technical.)

(B) is irrelevant. Winds are not said to be affected by the types of gases found in the atmosphere. They're affected by temperature differentials.

(C) does not help. It's consistent with the observation of stronger winds, but if offers no explanation *why* this would be the case. That's what the question is asking for.

(D) is an Irrelevant Comparison. The mystery is not about the number of planets that have stronger winds. The mystery is about why any planet (Jupiter in particular) would have stronger winds in the first place, and this offers no explanation for that.

(E) is Out of Scope. Other planets do not factor into the mystery here. Besides, the mystery is not that Jupiter or any other distant planet has winds at all. The mystery is why Jupiter has *stronger* winds, despite being so far from the Sun.

9. (C) Flaw

Step 1: Identify the Question Type

The correct answer will describe how the argument is "vulnerable to criticism," making this a Flaw question.

Step 2: Untangle the Stimulus

The author concludes ([s]o) that there's an increasing number of animals that can reproduce through parthenogenesis. The evidence is that scientists are now more interested in parthenogensis and have started finding more animals that reproduce that way.

Step 3: Make a Prediction

Just because scientists are observing parthenogenesis more often doesn't mean it's happening more often. It's possible that the animals they're learning about (e.g., sharks and Komodo dragons) have always reproduced by parthenogenesis, but scientists just didn't know about it because they weren't interested in studying that. The author assumes otherwise—that animals weren't reproducing this way when scientists weren't studying it as much. The correct answer will expose this flawed assumption.

Step 4: Evaluate the Answer Choices

(C) is correct, describing the author's assumption that parthenogenesis didn't happen in the past because scientists didn't see it happen (they ignored its occurrence).

(A) is Out of Scope. The argument is not concerned with having a real understanding of parthenogenesis.

(B) describes the commonly tested flaw of confusing correlation with causation. However, the author is not stating or implying that any one thing caused another to happen. The author is merely arguing that something is happening more often than it used to.

(D) is Out of Scope. There are no two situations. Perhaps this might refer to sharks and Komodo dragons, but they are the same in that they reproduce through parthenogenesis. Any other differences are irrelevant to the argument.

(E) is Out of Scope. The quality of the research is not addressed in this argument.

10. (C) Principle (Identify/Strengthen)

Step 1: Identify the Question Type

The question asks for a principle, making this an Identify the Principle question. Further, that principle will "help to justify the reasoning" given, which means this will also work like a Strengthen question.

Step 2: Untangle the Stimulus

The physician starts off with a recommendation, which is the conclusion: Psychologists without medical degrees should not prescribe medications. The evidence is that training in psychology requires just a few hundred hours of education, while medical degrees require years of training.

Step 3: Make a Prediction

The physician's argument is entirely based on how much time one spends getting trained. Essentially, the physician does not find the relatively short training period for psychology to be enough for prescribing medications. The author must be acting on the principle that prescribing medications should only be allowed by people who have had ample training (i.e., years).

Step 4: Evaluate the Answer Choices

(C) is correct, justifying the suggestion that those without medical degrees (i.e., those without years of training) should be denied the ability to give prescriptions.

(A) is a Distortion. Even if it's okay for psychologists with medical degrees to write prescriptions, that does not justify the argument that those *without* medical degrees should *not*. Maybe they could be allowed to write prescriptions, too.

(B) is a Distortion. If anything, this suggests that it's really the clinical psychology training that's important. In that case, this offers no support for denying psychologists the ability to write prescriptions.

(D) is a Distortion. The author is suggesting that extended training is necessary, not sufficient. The author is arguing that you can't prescribe medications without the years of training, not that anyone with that training automatically can prescribe medications. Furthermore, even if the physician's argument is understood as years of training are sufficient, that doesn't mean it's the minimal sufficient amount. Perhaps the hundreds of hours clinical psychologists spend are sufficient too.

(E) is a Distortion. The author is not telling psychologists to go through all of that training. The author is just telling them not to prescribe medications unless they do go through that training.

11. (C) Parallel Flaw

Step 1: Identify the Question Type
The correct answer will be an argument that illustrates the flaw in the stimulus "by parallel reasoning," making this a Parallel Flaw question.

Step 2: Untangle the Stimulus
By rejecting what some people argue, the lobbyist is trying to claim that exhaust emissions are not a health risk. The evidence is that, despite an increase in exhaust emissions, overall health has improved.

Step 3: Make a Prediction
Even if health has improved overall, that doesn't mean exhaust emissions are safe. Perhaps health levels would be even higher without those emissions. The author overlooks that possibility, and the correct answer will commit the same error. It will show how a situation has gotten better (health has improved) despite the increase of a potentially harmful factor (emissions). It will then conclude that the harmful factor doesn't affect the situation, overlooking how the harmful factor could still be making things worse than they might otherwise be.

Step 4: Evaluate the Answer Choices
(C) is correct. It shows how a situation has gotten better (traffic accidents overall are down) despite the increase of a potentially harmful factor (cell phones). Then, it concludes that the harmful factor doesn't affect the situation (cell phones aren't dangerous), overlooking how the accident rate could be even lower if cell phones weren't around.

(A) does not match. The author doesn't provide a harmful factor that contributes to a situation, so there's no suggestion that the situation got better despite an increase in any such factor.

(B) does not match. This argument is certainly flawed (as smoking could still be harmful even if it doesn't harm everyone), but not for the same reason. There's no increase in smoking and no suggestion that any situation has gotten better.

(D) does not match. The argument is flawed (skydiving could still be dangerous), but not in the same way. This argument is

not about a potentially harmful factor that the author claims is not a problem despite its increase.

(E) does not match. This does not claim that a supposed risk is actually okay. This just claims that the risk is still present, but there are ways to handle it should it happen.

12. (B) Assumption (Sufficient)

Step 1: Identify the Question Type
The correct answer will logically complete the argument, "if [it] is assumed," making this a Sufficient Assumption question.

Step 2: Untangle the Stimulus
The author concludes (*so*) that the recently discovered fossil is not evidence of birds evolving from dinosaurs. The evidence is that the fossil is composed of several bones scattered around the discovery site, and a fossil needs to be from a single animal to be evidence of birds evolving from dinosaurs.

Step 3: Make a Prediction
If the fossil has to be from a single animal to qualify as evidence, then the author's assertion that it *doesn't* qualify suggests that it's *not* from a single animal. However, the evidence doesn't say that. The evidence says the fossil is a composite of various bones. However, those bones could still have come from the same animal. The author assumes otherwise, that the composite did not come from a single animal.

Step 4: Evaluate the Answer Choices
(B) is correct. If composites are made from more than one animal, then it cannot satisfy the one-animal requirement and thus cannot be considered evidence of birds evolving from dinosaurs, just as the author concludes.

(A) is Out of Scope. The argument is dependent on what is actually true about the fossil, not what anybody believes or who holds that belief.

(C) is Out of Scope. The presence of other fossils that provide evidence of birds evolving from dinosaurs does nothing to confirm whether or not the newly discovered fossil can also provide such evidence.

(D) is Out of Scope. The quality of preservation plays no role in this argument.

(E) is Out of Scope. While this raises some ethical questions, such questions are irrelevant in deciding whether or not the fossils provide evidence of birds evolving from dinosaurs.

13. (A) Flaw

Step 1: Identify the Question Type
The question asks for something that "describes a flaw" in the argument, making this a Flaw question.

Step 2: Untangle the Stimulus
The author concludes ([S]o) that Justine has syndrome Q. The evidence is that the result of Justine's test was positive, and everyone with the syndrome yields a positive result when tested.

Step 3: Make a Prediction
This is a prime example of confusing sufficiency and necessity. The trigger word *whenever* in the second sentence indicates Formal Logic: Whenever someone has the syndrome, the test result is positive.

$$\text{If } \begin{array}{c} \textbf{\textit{have}} \\ \textbf{\textit{syndrome Q}} \end{array} \quad \rightarrow \quad \textbf{\textit{test positive}}$$

However, that is not the same as saying anyone who tests positive must have the syndrome. That would be improperly reversing the logic. Everyone who has the syndrome tests positive, but it's possible that people who don't have the syndrome accidentally test positive, too. The author overlooks that possibility, and that's what the correct answer will describe.

Step 4: Evaluate the Answer Choices
(A) is correct. The logic is that everyone with the syndrome tests positive, not that everyone who tests positive has the syndrome.

(B) is not a flaw. The author does make a claim about the test's accuracy: Those with the syndrome will test positive. However, scientific justification has been made ("research has shown"). The author then uses what the research has shown to inaccurately make a specific claim about Justine.

(C) is a Distortion. This suggests the author believes that not having the syndrome and not testing positive are the same thing. The author does not make such an error. The author just assumes that a positive result is a sure indicator of the syndrome.

(D) is not accurate. First off, there's no suggestion that the research involved an "arbitrary group of individuals." Moreover, the author does not make a similar claim when arguing about Justine. The claim about the group is that having the syndrome means you'll get a positive test result. The claim about Justine is reversed: Getting a positive test result means she has the syndrome.

(E) is a 180. It's suggested that the test *does* provide reliable results in the presence of syndrome Q. There's no suggestion that any results are not reliable.

14. (D) Inference
Step 1: Identify the Question Type
The question asks for something that is "strongly supported" by the given information, making this an Inference question.

Step 2: Untangle the Stimulus
The historian starts by noting how radio stations used to play only songs that were three minutes or shorter. Rock musicians and critics were not happy, claiming that this stifled creativity and that rock music wasn't really artistic until that barrier was lifted. The historian, *however*, argues otherwise, claiming that rock music is not suited to longer songs and that lifting the barrier resulted in aimless, structurally inferior songs.

Step 3: Make a Prediction
The entire stimulus hinges on a difference of opinion. Some people (musicians and critics) dislike the three-minute barrier and feel that removing it made music better. The historian argues that removing the barrier led to overlong, aimless songs. As the question asks for something supported by the historian's claim, expect the correct answer to be in favor of the three-minute barrier.

Step 4: Evaluate the Answer Choices
(D) is correct, as the historian claims that removing the barrier led to inferior songs, suggesting that the barrier may have had some benefit, after all.

(A) is not supported. Even if rock musicians are correct and creativity is limited to some degree, rock music could still be a great outlet for expressing some creative ideas.

(B) is Out of Scope. The historian does not dispute the claim that rock music became artistic when the songs were longer. The historian just feels they lost structure. There's no stated or implied need to borrow from other musical styles.

(C) is Out of Scope. The historian does not mention any need for discipline, nor does the historian compare the need for discipline in rock music to that in other forms of music.

(E) is Extreme and Out of Scope. The historian only addresses the length and structure of rock songs, not what type of musicians would make the *best* rock music.

15. (C) Method of Argument
Step 1: Identify the Question Type
The question asks what the argument does, rather than what it says, making this a Method of Argument question.

Step 2: Untangle the Stimulus
The author starts by presenting what some historians argue. They claim that the recipes of Apicius reflect the way wealthy ancient Romans cooked. However, the author argues that the historians may be too hasty in their conclusion. As evidence, the author notes how there are very few other ancient recipes for comparison, so Apicius's recipes may not have been typical, just like modern chefs don't necessarily use typical recipes.

Step 3: Make a Prediction

It's important to note that the author is not saying the historians are wrong. The author is just claiming that their evidence is insufficient—they're reacting too hastily. The correct answer will indicate the author's hesitancy without being extreme and outright contradicting the historians. Moreover, the author draws a comparison between Apicius and modern chefs, so the correct answer is likely to mention that, too.

Step 4: Evaluate the Answer Choices

(C) is correct. The author does have a problem with the historians' rash judgment, and an analogy to modern chefs is made to support the author's criticism of those historians.

(A) is Extreme. The author definitely points out the insufficient evidence, but that's as far as the author goes. The author never goes so far as to actually *reject* the historians' claim (i.e., say the historians are actually wrong). Also, the author's conclusion is not based just on lack of evidence, but *also* on an analogy to modern chefs.

(B) is a 180. The author is criticizing the historians, not supporting their view.

(D) is a Distortion. The author does not use the historians' view, as the author's intention is to criticize that view. Moreover, the modern comparison is used to support the author's conclusion, not the other way around.

(E) is a Distortion. The conclusion is only a criticism of the historians' view. Any comparison to modern chefs is used as evidence, not as part of the conclusion.

16. (E) Inference

Step 1: Identify the Question Type

The correct answer will be "strongly supported by the information" provided, making this an Inference question.

Step 2: Untangle the Stimulus

The author notes that wood can be preserved if it's waterlogged or desiccated, but normally it will disintegrate within 100–200 years. This is supposedly why it's hard to find remains of early wheeled vehicles. *However*, the author notes how archaeologists have found models of vehicles from the same time period made of ceramic, and these models are used as evidence regarding early vehicles.

Step 3: Make a Prediction

The phrase "[f]or this reason" in the second sentence is important. The author is claiming that wood's rapid rate of disintegration is the reason why so few early wheeled vehicles were found. The implication is that those vehicles were made of wood, and that's why the primary evidence of early vehicles comes from models made of materials that didn't disintegrate so quickly (e.g., ceramic). The correct answer will be consistent with this analysis.

Step 4: Evaluate the Answer Choices

(E) is correct, suggesting that most early vehicles were made of wood and not some material such as ceramic, which the still-preserved models indicate does not disintegrate as easily.

(A) is Out of Scope. There is no information about who made the models or the vehicles. Even if they were made in the same time period, they could have been created by different individuals.

(B) is not supported. It can't be determined how many such models were made of wood because the wood would have disintegrated by now. It's possible that most models were made of wood but only the ceramic ones remain for archaeologists to study.

(C) is not supported. The vehicle creators very well could have been aware that waterlogged or desiccated wood would be better preserved. They may have just chosen not to use such wood because it wouldn't make a good vehicle.

(D) is a 180. At least as it applies to wood, the author suggests that waterlogged or desiccated artifacts would last longer. Subsequently, if more of it lasts, it should be easier to find, not more difficult.

17. (C) Assumption (Necessary)

Step 1: Identify the Question Type

The question asks for an "assumption required by the argument," making this a Necessary Assumption question.

Step 2: Untangle the Stimulus

The author concludes (*therefore*) that fish released from experimental hatcheries are more likely to survive than fish released from traditional hatcheries. The evidence is that, when released from their flashier, more stimulating environment, the experimental hatchery fish are bolder in seeking out new environments and new foods to eat.

Step 3: Make a Prediction

The argument rests on Mismatched Concepts. The conclusion is about the survival rate of the fish, while the evidence is about their boldness in seeking out environments and food. The author must assume that these concepts are connected, i.e., boldness affects survival. Furthermore, there's no actual evidence of which fish survive longer. So, the author also assumes that the traditional hatchery fish don't last as long in the wild as the experimental hatchery fish do.

Step 4: Evaluate the Answer Choices

(C) is correct, confirming that traditional hatchery fish struggle to survive while also connecting boldness to survival. Using the Denial Test, if traditional hatchery fish do *not* die from timidness (i.e., lack of boldness), then that severs the link between boldness and survival and destroys the assumption that traditional hatchery fish struggle to survive. This answer cannot be denied and thus must be assumed.

(A) is Out of Scope. The argument is about survival, not economic feasibility.

(B) is not necessary. Even if the quality of the environment did have a major impact on survival, boldness could still also play a major role. The author's argument can stand whether this claim is true or not.

(D) is a Distortion. The author only claims that the experimental hatchery fish are bolder in trying new foods. That doesn't mean the traditional hatchery fish won't try new foods at all or are not getting the variety they need.

(E) is Extreme. The wild habitats don't *always* have to be visually stimulating. Even if the wild habitat is dull, the stimulating environment of the hatchery can still provide a survival advantage.

18. (E) Flaw

Step 1: Identify the Question Type
The correct answer will describe why the argument is "vulnerable to criticism," making this a Flaw question. Moreover, the question stem indicates that the flaw will involve an overlooked possibility.

Step 2: Untangle the Stimulus
The author concludes ("[t]his shows") that people start the day happy, become less happy in the afternoon, then get happier again in the evening. The evidence is that positive words appear on social media a lot in the morning, less in the afternoon, and a lot again in the evening.

Step 3: Make a Prediction
The author assumes that the appearance of words on social media is indicative of how individuals' moods change throughout the day. The author is overlooking a lot of alternative ways to interpret the social media data, so predicting the exact one may be challenging. In a case like this, it might be better to have a broad prediction and look for an answer that shows how the words on social media throughout the day do not necessarily reflect individual moods throughout the day.

Step 4: Evaluate the Answer Choices
(E) is correct. What if the people who post in the evening are mostly different from those who post in the morning? In that case, you'd have some people who post happy thoughts in the morning, get unhappier in the afternoon, then stop posting. Additionally, you'd have other people who don't post in the morning, are unhappy in the afternoon, but are happy in the evening. This could indicate two completely different mood patterns, contradicting the author's conclusion. So, this is something the author overlooks.

(A) is an Irrelevant Comparison. The argument is not about how moods change from day to day. The argument is about how moods change during any given day. Even if moods are overall higher during the weekend, the daily trend of happy to less happy to more happy could still apply.

(B) is irrelevant. Even if there are a lot of exceptional people who don't use positive or negative words, they could still be in the minority and the mood-based posts could still indicate a more typical trend.

(C) is an Irrelevant Comparison. Even if people use different words in other forms of communication (e.g., phone calls or ... I don't know ... semaphore), the author can still claim that social media posts are the true indicator of people's moods.

(D) is a Distortion. This confuses numbers and percentages. Saying that "the use of words associated with positive moods is common" suggests a high proportion or percentage of positive posts (e.g., 75% positive), not necessarily a large number of such words. Even if there are many more morning posts than evening posts, the author's argument could still stand about the general proportion of moods throughout the day.

19. (E) Assumption (Necessary)

Step 1: Identify the Question Type
The question directly asks for an assumption, and one that the "argument requires," making this a Necessary Assumption question.

Step 2: Untangle the Stimulus
The economist starts off with the conclusion: A maximum wage law (one that prevents an excessive salary gap between executives and lower-paid employees) would protect many lowest-paid employees from having their wages cut. The evidence is that a maximum wage law would remove the incentive for cutting wages to increase profits.

Step 3: Make a Prediction
The law would take away *one* incentive for cutting people's wages. However, the economist overlooks the possibility that executives might still cut employee wages for other reasons, even if the law is enacted. To conclude that the lowest-paid employees are safe from wage cuts, the economist must assume otherwise—that executives won't cut those wages for other reasons.

Step 4: Evaluate the Answer Choices
(E) is correct. When translated, this matches the prediction: At least some executives (one or more) won't cut the wages of the lowest-paid employees. The Denial Test confirms that this is necessary. What if this weren't true and there were no such executives? What if every executive says, "You know what? We're going to cut wages anyway." Then the author's argument is invalid. A lot of wages will still get cut. So, the

author must assume otherwise—there must be some executives that won't cut the wages.

(A) is Extreme. It need not be *all* the corporations that have a CEO making 50 times (or more) what the lowest -paid employee makes. Even if there are a few exceptions, the economist's argument that "the wages of *many* ... would be protected" by the maximum wage law holds.

(B) is a 180. If some executives who cut wages are already making less than 50 times the lowest salary in the company, then the new law wouldn't affect them. So, the law would not really provide a reason for them for them to stop cutting wages or an impediment to prevent them from doing so.

(C) is Extreme and a Distortion. This claims that the maximum wage law needs to be in place to raise people's wages. The economist is not saying the maximum wage law is necessary. Further, the economist is arguing about preventing wage cuts, not raising wages.

(D) is a Distortion. The author is not assuming that executives would only change the wages of low-paid employees to increase the executives' salaries. The executives may still cut the salaries to improve overall corporate profits. So, per the Denial Test, if the executives could not increase their own salaries by cutting the employees' salaries, but they would still *sometimes* change the wages (perhaps even for the good), then that does not crush the argument for a maximum wage law. The law would still serve as a disincentive to undertaking the practice to increase executive salaries.

20. (D) Weaken

Step 1: Identify the Question Type
The question asks for something that "weakens the argument," making this a Weaken question.

Step 2: Untangle the Stimulus
The author concludes ([*t*]*hus*) that consuming triglyceride-increasing foods and beverages can lead to heart disease. The evidence is that people with high triglyceride levels in the blood tend to have more heart attacks, and triglyceride levels rise when they're not metabolized properly. So, it's a causal chain of factors:

If   triglycerides inadequately metabolized   →   increase in triglycerides   →   more prone to heart disease

Step 3: Make a Prediction
The fatty foods, sugary snacks, and alcohol may increase triglycerides, but the first sentence puts the blame for high triglyceride levels on inadequate metabolizing. The author

must assume that the fatty foods, sugary snacks, and alcohol can impact the metabolism of triglycerides enough to reach the 1 milligram per milliliter level that makes people prone to heart attacks. To weaken the argument, the correct answer should show how those foods and beverages are not enough by themselves and/or that the metabolism is actually impacted by something else.

Step 4: Evaluate the Answer Choices
(D) is correct. This suggests a reversal in the causation—that metabolism is affected by existing heart conditions. So, consuming those foods and beverages might not be an issue if one does not already have heart problems.

(A) is an Irrelevant Comparison. This only mentions the fat content of the diets. If the sedentary people have high-sugar diets or drink a lot of alcohol, then that could still explain the higher rate of heart diseases, thus staying consistent with the author's argument. The exercise may also mitigate the risks caused by the high-fat diet, so this does not weaken the author's argument.

(B) is Out of Scope. The argument is only about the impact on heart diseases, not other diseases.

(C) is a 180. This strengthens the connection between triglycerides and the foods in question, thus making it more likely that those foods are causing problems.

(E) is Out of Scope or a possible 180. This choice is immaterial because it does not explicitly make or sever any connection between triglycerides and heart disease. If anything, it suggests that health-conscious people might already recognize that fat, sugar, and alcohol are problems for their hearts, which would be consistent with the author's view.

21. (E) Assumption (Necessary)

Step 1: Identify the Question Type
The question asks for an "assumption the argument requires," making this a Necessary Assumption question.

Step 2: Untangle the Stimulus
The author concludes that aerobic exercise helps people handle psychological stress. The evidence involves an experiment in which one group took aerobic exercise classes and a second group took weight-training classes. After three months, the people in the first group experienced lower stress when answering a math question.

Step 3: Make a Prediction
To conclude that aerobic exercise was a factor, the author must assume that the people in the first group got more aerobic exercise than people in the second group. Surely, the first group got aerobic exercise in their aerobic exercise classes. But what about the people in the second group? Even though they attended weight-training classes, does that mean they got less aerobic exercise? Couldn't they have

gotten just as much aerobic exercise from their classes or some other source? The author overlooks that possibility and assumes otherwise—that the people in the first group did, in fact, get more aerobic exercise overall.

Step 4: Evaluate the Answer Choices

(E) is correct. If both groups got the same amount of aerobic exercise, then there's no reason to suggest that aerobic exercise had anything to do with the different stress levels. The author must assume the aerobic exercise levels were different.

(A) is Extreme. The participants didn't have to *fully* benefit from the exercise. As long as stress levels went down, the argument still stands.

(B) is Out of Scope. It doesn't matter whether or not people in the first group did anything else. As long as they got more aerobic exercise, the argument still stands.

(C) is an Irrelevant Comparison. The argument is about the comparison between one group and another, not one group before and after the experiment.

(D) is also an Irrelevant Comparison. It's not about how difficult the math seemed, but how much stress the volunteers felt. If anything, this could weaken the argument by providing an alternative explanation for the lower stress levels. It may not have been the aerobic exercise. Perhaps the first group was just better at math.

22. (E) Weaken

Step 1: Identify the Question Type

The question asks for something that "undermines the reasoning" given, making this a Weaken question.

Step 2: Untangle the Stimulus

The author concludes that office furniture is not designed to promote workers' health. The evidence is that office workers who sit for long hours experience more lower-back injuries than people who do physical work that places stress on the lower back.

Step 3: Make a Prediction

The author assumes that the sitting and the office furniture are the primary factors responsible for the difference in lower-back injuries. However, the author fails to consider other factors. Maybe there's something else that causes office workers lower-back pain, or maybe the people who do physical labor do something that counteracts the stress on the lower back. To weaken this argument, the correct answer should indicate another significant factor that could account for the different injury rates.

Step 4: Evaluate the Answer Choices

(E) is correct. If physical activity is so effective at preventing lower-back injuries, that could explain the difference. It's not that the office furniture is unhelpful to office workers; it's just

that the physical workers are acting in a way that is even more helpful.

(A) is a 180. If out-of-work experiences are the same, then that makes it more likely that something at work (perhaps the office furniture) is responsible for the greater rate of injuries.

(B) is Out of Scope. It doesn't matter what insurance companies are willing to do. The argument concerns the source of any injuries and whether office furniture played any role.

(C) is irrelevant. The physical workers may be encouraged to use stress-relieving techniques, but that doesn't mean they actually use those techniques. And even if they did, this is not enough to show that these techniques would relieve stress enough to account for such a low rate of injuries compared to those who don't perform such physical activity.

(D) is a 180. If the injuries occur on the job, that just makes it more likely that the office furniture could be responsible.

23. (A) Paradox

Step 1: Identify the Question Type

The correct answer will "help to explain" something, making this a Paradox question.

Step 2: Untangle the Stimulus

There's a national park designed to protect birds. However, the author notes that more birds are found in unprotected areas outside the park than in similar areas within the park.

Step 3: Make a Prediction

Paraphrase the mystery as a question. If the park is meant to protect the birds, why are there more birds in the unprotected areas outside the park? There are two possible explanations. Either there's something different inside the park that is bad for the birds, or there is something different outside the park that is beneficial to the birds. The correct answer will provide one of these two differences.

Step 4: Evaluate the Answer Choices

(A) is correct. If the park has a lot of protected moose that eat the birds' food, then that would have a negative effect on the birds. This suggests that the birds would be better off outside the park, hence leading to greater numbers there.

(B) is an Irrelevant Comparison. While this does point out a difference between areas inside and outside the park, it provides no logical connection between reptiles and birds. Thus, there's no explanation why the difference in reptile population would have any impact on the different number of birds.

(C) does not help. This is consistent with the findings, suggesting that birds are, indeed, leaving the protected areas. However, it doesn't offer any explanation *why* they're doing so.

(D) is 180. If the two areas have pretty much the same environment, that just makes it more unusual that one area (the unprotected one, no less) has so many more birds.

(E) is a 180. If the birds outside the park are also endangered, then they should be afforded protection within the park, so it's even more unusual that they're found in greater numbers outside the park.

24. (B) Flaw

Step 1: Identify the Question Type
The question asks why the "argument is flawed," making this a Flaw question.

Step 2: Untangle the Stimulus
The author concludes ([c]*learly*) that university graduates are more likely to have a cat than a dog. The evidence provides some statistics: 47% of homes with cats have at least one university grad, while only 38% of homes with dogs have at least one university grad.

Step 3: Make a Prediction
The author is confusing percentages and numbers. While a greater percentage of cat homes have university grads, that doesn't mean a greater *number* of cat homes have university grads. It's possible that there are a lot more dog homes, and 38% of a larger number can be greater than 47% of a lower number (e.g., 38% of 100,000 is 38,000 homes while 47% of 10,000 is only 4,700 homes). The author assumes the numbers of homes are roughly equal, and the correct answer will point out this mathematical error.

Step 4: Evaluate the Answer Choices
(B) is correct, pointing out the author's assumption that there aren't a lot more dogs.

(A) is a Distortion. Even if there are homes with both pets, the statistics wouldn't change.

(C) is Out of Scope. The argument is about people who do have a university degree. People without such a degree have no bearing on the argument.

(D) is Out of Scope. The argument is not about who chooses the pet, but about whether or not the pet is there.

(E) is Out of Scope. The author's conclusion is carefully worded to just suggest a correlation (the numbers are more likely to align a certain way). The author never goes so far as to suggest that having a university degree *causes* them to buy the pet.

25. (C) Parallel Reasoning

Step 1: Identify the Question Type
The question asks for an argument that is "parallel in its reasoning" to the argument in the stimulus, making this a Parallel Reasoning question.

Step 2: Untangle the Stimulus
The author concludes ([t]*herefore*) that Keeler must have notified the press. The evidence is that Keeler and Greene were the only people who could have done so, and Keeler had a motive while Greene did not.

Step 3: Make a Prediction
The argument is structured around eliminating one alternative in favor of another based on motive. The correct answer should have the same structure. It will provide two people who could have performed an action and conclude that it must be the one who had a motive, not the one without a motive.

Step 4: Evaluate the Answer Choices
(C) is correct. There are two people (Helms and Lapinski) who could have tampered with the equipment, and the author concludes that it must be the one who had a motive (Helms) and not the one who didn't (Lapinski).

(A) does not match. This does have two people who could have performed an action. However, the conclusion is based on one person claiming to have performed the action in the past, not by eliminating the person without a motive.

(B) does not match. *Both* people here had motives. However, Whitequill also had a countervailing motive *not* to perform the act (too afraid). That's not parallel to the stimulus.

(D) does not match. This argument *rejects* the person with a motive because the motive didn't apply (nobody wanted to take credit).

(E) does not match. This chooses one person based on supporting evidence. There's no elimination of the second person for not having similar motives, or in this case qualifications. Furthermore, **(E)**'s conclusion of "will probably" is a likely prediction, but the conclusion of the stimulus is an absolute claim about the past.

Section IV: Logic Games

Game 1: Weekly Department Store Sales

Q#	Question Type	Correct	Difficulty
1	Partial Acceptability	C	★
2	"If" / Must Be True	B	★★
3	"If" / Could Be True	D	★
4	"If" / Completely Determine	A	★
5	"If" / Must Be True	A	★
6	Rule Substitution	E	★★★

Game 2: Antiques Fair Information Booths

Q#	Question Type	Correct	Difficulty
7	Acceptability	A	★
8	"If" / Complete and Accurate List	A	★★
9	"If" / Must Be True	D	★
10	How Many	C	★
11	"If" / Could Be True	B	★★
12	"If" / Must Be True	D	★
13	Must Be False (CANNOT Be True)	D	★★

Game 3: Textbook Editors

Q#	Question Type	Correct	Difficulty
14	Acceptability	E	★
15	"If" / Could Be True	B	★
16	"If" / Could Be True	B	★★
17	"If" / Must Be True	D	★★
18	Must Be False (CANNOT Be True)	C	★★

Game 4: Art Exhibitions with Musical Performances

Q#	Question Type	Correct	Difficulty
19	Acceptability	B	★
20	"If" / Must Be True	B	★★
21	"If" / Could Be True	E	★★★
22	Must Be False (CANNOT Be True)	C	★★
23	"If" / Must Be True	D	★★★★

Game 1: Weekly Department Store Sales

Step 1: Overview

Situation: A department store holding weekly sales

Entities: Seven types of products (headphones, lamps, microwaves, printers, refrigerators, speakers, televisions)

Action: Strict Sequencing. Determine the order in which the products will be placed on sale.

Limitations: All seven products will go on sale, with exactly one product on sale each week. With seven weeks of sales, this will be standard one-to-one sequencing.

Step 2: Sketch

List the entities by initial, and set up a series of seven numbered slots.

Step 3: Rules

Rule 1 requires at least two weeks in between the headphones sale and the speakers sale. It does not say which sale will happen first, so be sure to consider both options. Also, because it says "at least" two weeks, set up two definite slots in between these sales, but also include an ellipsis to indicate that additional sales can be added in between.

$$\underline{H/S} \quad \underline{\quad} \quad \underline{\quad} \quad \ldots \quad \underline{S/H}$$

Rule 2 states that the sales of printers and speakers must be consecutive, but it does not say in which order. Draw both possible blocks to the side.

$$\boxed{PS} \; or \; \boxed{SP}$$

Rule 3 limits the sale of televisions to either the first or seventh week. Note this to the side ("T = 1 or 7"), or draw a T above (or below) the sketch with arrows pointing to the first and last slot.

Rule 4 provides some Formal Logic. If televisions are not on sale in the first week, then refrigerators are. By contrapositive, if refrigerators are not on sale in the first week, then televisions are. Instead of writing this logic out, consider what this logic really implies: If it's not one, it's the other, i.e., the first sale has to be either refrigerators or televisions. So, add "R/T" to the first slot.

Rule 5 provides a loose relationship: Lamps will be on sale before headphones.

$$L \ldots H$$

Step 4: Deductions

Despite a healthy number of rules and a bunch of duplicated entities, there are really no significant deductions in this game. Rules 3 and 4 seem to offer chances for Limited Options, especially given that they both mention televisions. However, it doesn't matter which week televisions go on sale. Neither option establishes any other sales. Furthermore, knowing if refrigerators are on sale the first week only confirms that televisions are on sale in the last week. It's likely not worth drawing out two full sketches for one minor deduction.

Rule 1 offers the next best chance for deductions, as both entities mentioned (headphones and speakers) are duplicated in Rules 2 and 5. However, there are too many open-ended questions (Which comes first, headphones or speakers? And exactly how far apart are they?), so there is no truly effective way to combine the information in these rules.

As further evidence that deductions can be lacking, take a glance at the question set. After the Acceptability question, four of the remaining five questions provide a New-"If" clause, which often suggests that deductions will be scarce. Instead, be confident with the rules. Take note of the duplicated entities (headphones, speakers, televisions) as they can be important. And finally, note that microwaves are never mentioned in the rules, making that entity a Floater.

Step 5: Questions

1. (C) Partial Acceptability

The question asks for one possible outcome, but only for the last four weeks (weeks 4, 5, 6, and 7), in order. That makes this a Partial Acceptability question. Start by going through the rules and eliminating choices that violate those rules. If any choices remain, consider what the first three weeks might contain for each choice to test them individually.

The only choice that lists both headphones and speakers, but that does not violate Rule 1, is **(D)**. **(B)** violates Rule 2 by having printers flanked by microwaves and headphones, leaving no consecutive spot for speakers. (Note that **(C)** and **(D)** are still valid because the third week is not listed, and that week could contain printers or speakers to create the necessary block.) **(D)** can be eliminated because it violates Rule 3 by placing televisions in the sixth week. Rule 4 may seem impossible to test, as none of the choices list the first week. However, **(E)** can be eliminated because it lists both refrigerators and televisions, which would make it impossible to put one of them first. Finally, **(A)** violates Rule 5 because it lists lamps, but there are no more weeks afterwards to put headphones on sale. That leaves **(C)** as the correct answer, which would produce this acceptable order:

$$\frac{R}{1} \quad \frac{L}{2} \quad \frac{S}{3} \quad \frac{P}{4} \quad \frac{M}{5} \quad \frac{H}{6} \quad \frac{T}{7}$$

2. (B) "If" / Must Be True

For this question, printers will be the fourth sale. In that case, speakers would have to be the third or fifth sale (Rule 2). However, Rule 1 will make it impossible to have the speakers fifth. If speakers were fifth, there wouldn't be enough room afterward for headphones. So, headphones would have to come before speakers. To be far enough away for Rule 1, headphones would have to be first or second. However, the first week has to be televisions or refrigerators (Rule 4), so headphones cannot be first. Headphones also cannot be second, because that would place lamps first (Rule 5), violating Rule 4. So, speakers cannot be fifth.

I)
$$\frac{R/T}{1} \quad \frac{}{2} \quad \frac{S}{3} \quad \frac{P}{4} \quad \frac{}{5} \quad \frac{}{6} \quad \frac{}{7}$$

II)
$$\frac{R/T}{1} \quad \frac{}{2} \quad \frac{}{3} \quad \frac{P}{4} \quad \frac{S}{5} \quad \frac{}{6} \quad \frac{}{7}$$

Speakers must be third, making **(B)** the correct answer. The remaining choices could be true, but need not be.

3. (D) "If" / Could Be True

For this question, headphones will be fifth. By Rule 1, there must be two sales in between headphones and speakers, so speakers can only be first or second. However, Rule 4 creates a lot of deductions by forcing the first sale to be refrigerators or televisions. It prevents speakers from being first, so they must be second. It then prevents printers from being first, so printers now have to be third (Rule 2). Finally, it prevents lamps from being first, so they have to be fourth (Rule 5).

$$\frac{R/T}{1} \quad \frac{S}{2} \quad \frac{P}{3} \quad \frac{L}{4} \quad \frac{H}{5} \quad \frac{}{6} \quad \frac{}{7}$$

The question asks about microwaves, which also cannot be first because of Rule 4. If microwaves are on sale earlier than anything else, they would have to be sold sixth. The seventh sale could then be either of the remaining entities: refrigerators or televisions. Only one is listed in the choices, making **(D)** the correct answer.

4. (A) "If" / Completely Determine

For this question, refrigerators are on sale in the first week. That means televisions must be on sale in the seventh week (Rule 3).

$$\frac{R}{1} \quad \frac{}{2} \quad \frac{}{3} \quad \frac{}{4} \quad \frac{}{5} \quad \frac{}{6} \quad \frac{T}{7}$$

The remaining entities can be arranged in many ways. The correct answer will limit the number of arrangements to just one. Eliminate any choice that allows for more than one outcome.

(A) places the headphones third. By Rule 1, the speakers could only be sixth (as there is not enough room before headphones, and televisions are taking up the seventh week). That would mean the printers would have to be fifth (Rule 2). Lamps would have to be second (Rule 5), leaving the microwaves for the fourth week.

$$\frac{R}{1} \quad \frac{L}{2} \quad \frac{H}{3} \quad \frac{M}{4} \quad \frac{P}{5} \quad \frac{S}{6} \quad \frac{T}{7}$$

That is a completely determined outcome, making **(A)** correct. For the record:

If the speakers were third, the printers could still be second or fourth. That eliminates **(B)**. If the lamps were fourth, the headphones could still be fifth or sixth. That eliminates **(C)**. If the microwaves were fourth, then nothing else could be placed with certainty. That eliminates **(D)**. If the headphones were sixth, the speakers could still be second or third. That eliminates **(E)**.

5. (A) "If" / Must Be True

For this question, the sixth sale will be speakers. To have at least two weeks between speakers and headphones, the headphones would have to be on sale third or earlier. However, Rule 4 prevents headphones from being the first sale. Furthermore, if headphones were the second sale, then lamps would have to be first (Rule 5), but that also violates Rule 4. So, headphones could only be the third sale. In that case, lamps would have to be second.

$$\frac{R/T}{1} \quad \frac{L}{2} \quad \frac{H}{3} \quad \frac{}{4} \quad \frac{}{5} \quad \frac{S}{6} \quad \frac{}{7}$$

The question asks about microwaves. The first three weeks are closed out, so microwaves have to be sold at some point after that. It cannot be determined whether the first week is refrigerators or televisions, but microwaves will definitely be sold after the lamps and the headphones. That makes **(A)** the correct answer.

6. (E) Rule Substitution

The correct answer to this question will be a new rule that could replace Rule 4 without changing anything. In other words, it will create the exact same restriction without adding any new restrictions. Rule 4 is the one that makes it such that refrigerators or televisions have to be first. The correct answer needs to reestablish that condition without changing anything else.

(A) would indeed, when combined with Rule 3, force the first week to be refrigerators or televisions. However, it would also force the last week to be refrigerators or televisions. That's a restriction the original rule did not create. By the original rules, refrigerators could be sold in any week. This is too restrictive, so eliminate **(A)**.

(B) is valid in the original sketch and conforms perfectly to Rule 3. However, what if refrigerators were *not* on sale in the first week? This rule provides no guidance in that case. Anything else could then be first, as long as televisions are sold in the seventh week. This fails to establish the restriction of the original rule. That eliminates **(B)**.

(C) puts a restriction on the seventh week that was not required by the original rules. Also, it fails to set the needed restriction on the first week. That eliminates **(C)**.

(D) puts a restriction on refrigerators that was not originally present. If televisions are on sale first, the original rules put no restriction on refrigerators. That eliminates **(D)**, leaving **(E)** as the correct answer.

For the record: **(E)** places refrigerators first if televisions are seventh. Televisions can only be first or seventh (Rule 3). Saying televisions are seventh is exactly the same as saying they're not first. So, this rule can be rewritten to read, "If televisions are not on sale during the first week, refrigerators must be on sale during the first week." That's exactly what the original rule stated.

Game 2: Antiques Fair Information Booths

Step 1: Overview

Situation: An antiques fair at a civics center

Entities: Six employees (including Frank and Gladys—who have moved on from their farm exhibition stint on PrepTest 38—as well as Hal, Keisha, Laura, Mike) and three booths (organizers, retailers, visitors)

Action: Distribution. Assign the employees to the booths.

Limitations: Each employee will be assigned to exactly one of the three booths, and there must be at least one employee at each booth.

Step 2: Sketch

List the employees by initial and set up a table with a column for each booth. Add one slot to start off each booth.

F G H K L M

org	ret	vis
—	—	—

Step 3: Rules

Rule 1 sets a numeric restriction. The retailers booth will have more employees than the visitors booth. That means a second slot can already be added to the retailers column. However, as the numbers can still change, it's also useful to make a note of this rule. Put a ">" in between the retailers and visitors columns.

Rule 2 prevents Frank and Keisha from being assigned to the visitors booth. Add "~F" and "~K" beneath that column.

Rule 3 prevents Gladys and Hal from being assigned to the organizers booth. Add "~G" and "~H" beneath that column.

Rule 4 creates a Block of Entities. Gladys and Mike will work together at the same booth.

Step 4: Deductions

Gladys is mentioned in Rules 3 and 4. Because Gladys must be with Mike (Rule 4), and Gladys can't be in the organizers booth (Rule 3), that means Mike can't be in the organizers booth either. With Gladys, Mike, and Hal (Rule 3) all eliminated from the organizers booth, that leaves only Frank, Keisha, and Laura available to be placed there. If the number of entities that *can* be in a slot equals or exceeds the number that *cannot* be there, it is typically better to note the rule affirmatively. Put "F/K/L" in the slot under the organizers booth.

With only six entities, the block in Rule 4 accounts for a third of the entities. As already deduced, Gladys and Mike are eliminated from the organizers booth, so the block of Gladys and Mike can only be assigned to the retailers booth or the visitors booth. Given the numeric restriction placed on those booths by Rule 1, it would be worthwhile testing out Limited Options.

In the first option, Gladys and Mike would be assigned to the retailers booth. Other employees could be assigned to that booth as well, and no other entities can be placed for sure. However, it's useful to note that the visitors booth is very restricted. With Frank and Keisha kicked out (Rule 2), that leaves only Hal and Laura for the visitors booth. One of them (if not both) must be there. So, add "H/L" to the visitors booth—with the recognition that it's possible to assign them both to that booth.

I)
org	ret	>	vis
F/K/L	G		H/L
	M		
~H			~F ~K

In the second option, Gladys and Mike would be assigned to the visitors booth. By Rule 1, the retailers booth would have to receive a third employee. That solidifies the numbers: one employee at the organizers booth, three at the retailers booth, and two at the visitors booth. With Gladys and Mike there, the visitors booth is complete. Hal cannot be assigned to the organizers booth (Rule 3), so Hal must be assigned to the retailers booth. The remaining entities (Frank, Keisha, and Laura) could be placed in any of the open spaces.

II)
org	ret	>	vis
F/K/L	H		G
	—		M
	—		

Step 5: Questions

7. (A) Acceptability

As with any standard Acceptability question, go through the rules one at a time and eliminate choices as they violate the rules.

(C) violates Rule 1 by assigning an equal number of people to the retailers and visitors booth. **(D)** violates Rule 2 by assigning Frank to the visitors booth. **(E)** violates Rule 3 by assigning Hal to the organizers booth. **(B)** violates Rule 4 by assigning Gladys and Mike to different booths. That leaves **(A)** as the correct answer.

8. (A) "If" / Complete and Accurate List

For this question, Frank and Keisha are not assigned to the organizers booth. By Rule 2, they also cannot be assigned to the visitors booth. That means they both must be assigned to the retailers booth. That leaves Gladys, Hal, Laura, and Mike. By Rule 3, Gladys and Hal cannot be assigned to the organizers booth. Because Gladys and Mike must be together, Mike cannot be assigned to the organizers booth. That leaves only Laura, and the organizers booth must get somebody. So, Laura must be assigned to the organizers booth.

org	ret > vis
L	F
	K

The remaining entities could be assigned to either the retailers or the visitors booth, but they don't matter. The question asks about Laura, who must be assigned to the organizers booth. That makes **(A)** the correct answer.

9. (D) "If" / Must Be True

For this question, the organizers booth will get more employees than the retailers booth, which in turn must get more employees than the visitors booth (Rule 1). This can only happen in Option I, and the only way those numbers work is to have one person assigned to the visitors booth, two to the retailers booth, and three to the organizers booth.

The organizers booth cannot include Gladys or Hal (Rule 3), and without Gladys, it cannot include Mike (Rule 4). That leaves Frank, Keisha, and Laura as the three employees assigned to the organizers booth. From there, Gladys and Mike must be together, so they will have to take the two spots at the retailers booth, leaving Hal as the lone employee at the visitors booth.

org >	ret >	vis
F	G	H
K	M	
L		

With the sketch complete, the employee at the visitors booth must be Hal, making **(D)** the correct answer.

10. (C) How Many

The question asks for the number of employees who are eligible to work at the organizers booth. They do not have to all work there at the same time. Just count all the people who *could* work there.

By Rule 3, Gladys and Hal cannot work at the organizers booth. And because Mike has to work with Gladys (Rule 4), Mike cannot work there either. With those three out, that leaves only three people who could: Frank, Keisha, and Laura.

Any of them seem possible. In fact, in the third question of the game, all of them are assigned to the organizers booth. So, the total number of employees available for the organizers booth is three, making **(C)** the correct answer.

11. (B) "If" / Could Be True

For this question, Hal is assigned to some booth with exactly one other employee. It cannot be the organizers booth (Rule 3). It also cannot be the retailers booth. After all, if Hal was there with only one other person, that would mean only one person is at the visitors booth (Rule 1). Then, there would be no place to place Gladys and Mike together (Rule 4); there would be only one open space in the retailers and the visitors booths, and Gladys cannot be assigned to the organizers booth (Rule 2).

So, Hal and the one other person would have to be assigned to the visitors booth. That puts two people there, so the retailers booth must have three people (Rule 1), leaving only one for the organizers booth. The only place with room for Gladys and Mike is the retailers booth. That leaves Frank, Keisha, and Laura. Frank and Keisha cannot be assigned to the visitors booth, so Laura must go there, and Frank and Keisha will be assigned to the organizers and retailers booth, in either order.

I)	org	ret >	vis
	F/K	G	H
		M	L
		K/F	

Note that, with Limited Options, this could only happen in Option I, as Option II has Hal in the retailers booth with two other people, not just one. At that point, Hal would have to be assigned to the visitors booth along with Laura, and the resulting sketch would look exactly the same as the one above. Either way, only **(B)** is possible and thus the correct answer.

12. (D) "If" / Must Be True

For this question, Hal and Laura will not be assigned to the visitors booth. By Rule 2, Frank and Keisha cannot be there, either. That leaves only Gladys and Mike, who must be together (Rule 4). So, Gladys and Mike are assigned to the visitors booth. By Rule 1, the retailers booth must now have three employees, leaving just one for the organizers booth. Because Hal cannot work at the organizers booth, Hal must be assigned to the retailers booth. Frank, Keisha, and Laura will occupy the three remaining slots.

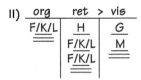

II)

org	ret	> vis
F/K/L	H	G
	F/K/L	M
	F/K/L	

Looking at the Limited Options, this could not occur in Option I, in which Hal or Laura must be assigned to the visitors booth. So, this could only happen in Option II, which produces the exact same sketch as the one above. Either way, the result is the same. Gladys and Mike are together at the visitors booth, making **(D)** the correct answer.

13. (D) Must Be False (CANNOT Be True)

The correct answer will be a list of people that cannot be assigned together in the retailers booth. The remaining four answers will all be possible.

Limited Options can help answer this question immediately. In Option I, the retailers booth has to include Gladys and Mike. In Option II, the retailers booth has to include Hal. So, one way or the other, the booth must include Gladys and Mike, or Hal. **(D)** has none of those three employees, and is thus impossible. That makes **(D)** correct.

Without Limited Options, previous work can be useful. The sketch for the fifth question shows a possible assignment of Frank, Mike, and Gladys, so that eliminates **(A)**. The sketch for the sixth question shows Hal in the retailers booth along with any two of Frank, Keisha, and Laura. That eliminates **(B)** and **(C)**. That would leave **(D)** and **(E)** to test. However, the second question could be most useful. In that sketch, Frank and Keisha are assigned to the retailers booth. When that happens, Laura is the only person left for the organizers booth and must be assigned there, not the retailers booth. So, that confirms **(D)** is impossible and thus the correct answer.

Game 3: Textbook Editors

Step 1: Overview

Situation: A publishing company preparing to publish new textbooks

Entities: Six textbooks (linguistics, macroeconomics, psychology, Russian, statistics, zoology) and three editors (Ferrer, Gupta, Hendricks)

Action: Distribution. Assign the textbooks to the editors.

Limitations: Each textbook will be edited by exactly one editor, and each editor will edit at least one textbook.

Step 2: Sketch

List the textbooks by the subject initials, and set up a table with a column for each editor. Start with one slot in each column.

```
      L M P R S Z
    Fer   Gup   Hen
    ___ | ___ | ___
```

Step 3: Rules

Rule 1 establishes at least one book for Ferrer: linguistics or zoology. Add "L/Z" to the Ferrer column. As the rule notes, Ferrer can also edit both, and there's no reason Ferrer can't edit other books, too.

Rule 2 presents some Formal Logic. If Gupta edits the macroeconomics book, that will be the only book he edits. By contrapositive, if Gupta edits any other book, then he can't edit the macroeconomics book.

$$\frac{Gup}{M} \rightarrow \frac{Gup}{\underline{M}}$$

$$\frac{Gup}{\substack{anything \\ besides \\ M}} \rightarrow \frac{\sim Gup}{M}$$

Rule 3 sets a numeric limit on Hendricks. Hendricks will edit exactly two books. Add a second book to the Hendricks column and close the column off.

Rule 4 restricts Hendricks from editing the macroeconomics book. Add "~M" under the Hendricks column.

Rule 5 creates a Block of Entities. The psychology and statistics textbooks will be edited by the same person.

Step 4: Deductions

Despite there being five rules, there's not much that can be deduced. Rule 5 provides a Block of Entities, but any of the three editors can receive that block without posing any problems. Rule 1 establishes linguistics or zoology with Ferrer, but it's not certain which one—it could be both—and neither outcome would produce any further deductions. There is a numeric component to the game, in that Hendricks is limited to two textbooks (Rule 3). However, Ferrer and Gupta can split the remaining four in any way: one for Ferrer and three for Gupta, three for Ferrer and one for Gupta, or two for both. Rules 3 and 4 both mention Hendricks, but Hendricks could still edit just about any pair of books that doesn't include macroeconomics.

The closest thing to a deduction comes with the other duplicated entity of the game: macroeconomics. It's mentioned in Rules 2 and 4. Hendricks can't edit it, so it must be either Ferrer or Gupta. If it was Gupta, Gupta would get just that one textbook, leaving Ferrer with three. If Ferrer edits macroeconomics—along with either linguistics or zoology (Rule 1)—Ferrer would not have room for the psychology and statistics block, but it could still go to Gupta or Hendricks. So, while drawing out the options is possible, they wouldn't produce a lot of valuable substance.

Instead, keep track of the significant duplicated entities (Hendricks and macroeconomics), note the Floater (Russian was never mentioned in the rules), and move ahead.

Step 5: Questions

14. (E) Acceptability

As with any Acceptability question, go through the rules one at a time, and eliminate choices as they violate the rules.

(B) violates Rule 1 by not giving Ferrer linguistics or zoology. **(C)** violates Rule 2 by giving Gupta macroeconomics, but not by itself. None of the choices violates Rule 3. **(D)** violates Rule 4 by giving Hendricks macroeconomics. **(A)** violates Rule 5 by giving psychology and statistics to different editors. That leaves **(E)** as the correct answer.

15. (B) "If" / Could Be True

For this question, Hendricks will edit Russian. That leaves Hendricks with only one more textbook to edit. It cannot be macroeconomics (Rule 4), and it cannot be the block of psychology and statistics (Rule 5). That leaves linguistics or zoology. Whichever one Hendricks edits, Ferrer will have to edit the other (Rule 1).

Fer	Gup	Hen
L/Z		R
		Z/L

That leaves the macroeconomics textbook and the psychology-statistics block. Gupta needs to edit something. Gupta can edit the macroeconomics book by itself (Rule 2), leaving the psychology-statistics block to Ferrer. Alternatively, Gupta can edit the psychology-statistics block and leave the macroeconomics book to Ferrer. Either way, **(B)** is the only choice possible, and thus the correct answer. For the record:

The linguistics and zoology textbooks are split between Ferrer and Hendricks, so that eliminates **(A)**, **(C)**, and **(D)**. Hendricks has Russian with linguistics or zoology, no psychology. That eliminates **(E)**.

16. (B) "If" / Could Be True

For this question, Gupta edits the zoology textbook. By Rule 1, Ferrer must then edit the linguistics textbook. With Gupta already editing zoology, Gupta cannot also edit macroeconomics (Rule 2). Additionally, Hendricks cannot edit macroeconomics (Rule 4). So, macroeconomics will be edited by Ferrer. That leaves Russian and the psychology-statistics block. Hendricks needs to edit two of those books, and the block cannot be split up. Therefore, Hendricks will edit psychology and statistics, leaving the Russian textbook for either Ferrer or Gupta.

Fer	Gup	Hen
L	Z	P
M		S

With that, only **(B)** is possible, and thus the correct answer.

17. (D) "If" / Must Be True

For this question, Hendricks edits the linguistics textbook. That leaves Ferrer with the zoology textbook (Rule 1). Hendricks needs one more textbook. It cannot be macroeconomics (Rule 4), and it cannot be the psychology-statistics block (Rule 5). That leaves the Russian textbook.

Fer	Gup	Hen
Z		L
		R

With Hendricks definitely editing the Russian textbook, **(D)** is the correct answer. **(A)**, **(B)**, and **(C)** all could be true. **(E)** must be false.

18. (C) Must Be False (CANNOT Be True)

The correct answer will be the one that cannot be true, i.e., must be false. The remaining answers will all be possible. With no major deductions, using previous work can save a lot of time on this question.

The sketch for the third question shows Hendricks editing psychology and statistics, so that could happen. That eliminates **(E)**. The sketch for the fourth question shows Hendricks editing linguistics and Russian. That eliminates **(D)**. In the sketch for the second question, Ferrer could get linguistics and could get the psychology-statistics block while Gupta gets macroeconomics. Thus, **(A)** is possible and can be eliminated. That leaves just two choices to test.

If Ferrer edits linguistics, Russian, and zoology, Gupta would need one textbook and Hendricks would need two. Hendricks would have to get the psychology-statistics block, leaving Gupta with macroeconomics.

Fer	Gup	Hen
L	M	P
R		S
Z		

That's acceptable, so **(B)** can be eliminated. That means **(C)** is the correct answer. For the record:

If Gupta edits psychology, statistics, and Russian, Ferrer would still need one book and Hendricks would need two. Ferrer would edit linguistics or zoology (Rule 1), but that would leave Hendricks with macroeconomics, violating Rule 4. This is impossible, confirming that **(C)** is the correct answer.

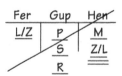

Game 4: Art Exhibitions with Musical Performances

Step 1: Overview

Situation: An art gallery holding weeklong art exhibitions

Entities: Five artists (Jackson, Katz, Lu, Norales, Odede) and five musicians (Timmons, Vega, Wilson, Yoder, Zheng)

Action: Strict Sequencing. Determine the order in which the artists will have their exhibitions and in which the musicians will perform—sequencing on two levels. These sequences will occur simultaneously, as each exhibition will feature one artist and one musician. Some might classify this game as a Hybrid of Sequencing (order the artists) along with either Matching or Distribution (assign the musicians). Technically, those game types operate a bit differently, but the specific label is not crucial here. Whatever it's called, the sketch would likely be the same (two rows of five slots), and that will ultimately be more important.

Limitations: There are five exhibitions, each with one artist and one musician. Each artist and each musician will be assigned to just one exhibition. So, this is just one-to-one sequencing for two concurrent sequences.

Step 2: Sketch

Set up two rows of numbered slots. Next to one row, list the artists by initial. Next to the second row, list the musicians by initial. To avoid confusion, use uppercase initials for one group and lowercase initials for the other.

	1	2	3	4	5
J K L N O	__	__	__	__	__
t v w y z	__	__	__	__	__

Step 3: Rules

Rule 1 provides loose sequencing for three of the artists: Jackson at some point before Katz, who is at some point before Lu.

$$J...K...L$$

Rule 2 provides loose sequencing for three of the musicians: Timmons before Vega, who will be before Wilson.

$$t...v...w$$

Rule 3 prevents Wilson from performing in the fourth week. Draw "~w" under the fourth column of the sketch.

Rule 4 states that one exhibition cannot contain the musician Yoder with the artist Norales. Make a note of this to the side.

Rule 5 creates a Block of Entities for one exhibition. It will contain the artist Odede with the musician Zheng.

Step 4: Deductions

The rules don't offer a lot of useful information. The block of Odede and Zheng can occur at any point in the sequencing. No entities are established in the sketch. There are no major numerical concerns. And the only entity duplicated in the rules is Wilson, who cannot perform at the fourth exhibition (Rule 3) but must perform after Timmons and Vega (Rule 2). Thus, Wilson could only perform at the third or fifth exhibition. If Wilson performed at the third exhibition, Timmons and Vega would have to perform at the first and second exhibition, respectively. However, nothing else could be established for certain, and no major deductions could be drawn if Wilson performed at the fifth exhibition. Thus, drawing out the two options would not provide a lot of value. This game will rely much more on confidence with the rules and building sketches based on the New-"If" questions.

Step 5: Questions

19. (B) Acceptability

As with any Acceptability question, go through the rules one at a time and test them against the choices. As the rules are violated, eliminate the choices until only one acceptable choice remains.

(C) violates Rule 1 by having Katz first without Jackson beforehand. None of the choices violates Rule 2. **(A)** violates Rule 3 by having Wilson in the fourth week. **(E)** violates Rule 4 by assigning Norales and Yoder together. **(D)** violates Rule 5 by assigning Odede and Zheng to different weeks. That leaves **(B)** as the correct answer.

20. (B) "If" / Must Be True

For this question, Vega will perform in the third week. Wilson must perform in a later week (Rule 2), but cannot perform in the fourth week (Rule 3). So, Wilson must perform in the fifth week, making **(B)** the correct answer. The remaining choices all could be, but not must be, true.

1	2	3	4	5
__	__	__	__	__
__	__	v	__	w

21. (E) "If" / Could Be True

This question creates two blocks: Timmons with Jackson, and Vega with Katz. Along with the block of Odede and Zheng (Rule 5), that's three exhibitions with the people scheduled. The remaining two exhibitions will feature artists Lu and Norales and musicians Wilson and Yoder. However, by Rule 4, Yoder cannot be assigned with Norales. So, Yoder will play at Lu's exhibition, pairing up Wilson with Norales.

The people at all five exhibitions are settled. Now, consider the order. By Rules 1 and 2, the Jackson-Timmons exhibition must occur before the Katz-Vega exhibition. Those will be followed by both the Lu-Yoder exhibition (Rule 1) and the Norales-Wilson exhibition (Rule 2), in either order—as long as Wilson is not fourth (Rule 3). The Odede-Zheng exhibition can occur in any week.

With that, only **(E)** is possible, as Zheng can perform in any week. For the record:

Jackson needs to precede Katz, Lu, and Norales, and thus could not be in the third week. That eliminates **(A)**. Norales is with Wilson, who cannot be fourth. That eliminates **(B)**. Vega needs to precede Yoder and Wilson, and thus could not be in the fourth week. That eliminates **(C)**, and Yoder has to come after Timmons and Vega, and thus could not be in the second week. That eliminates **(D)**.

22. (C) Must Be False (CANNOT Be True)

The question asks for two people who cannot be scheduled for the same exhibition. The remaining pairs will all be possible. Using sketches from other questions can be very useful here. For the third question, Norales and Wilson were scheduled in the same week, so that eliminates **(E)**. In the last question of the game, the sketch reveals that either Jackson or Norales could be scheduled with Vega, eliminating **(A)** and **(D)**. That sketch also shows that Katz and Yoder can be together. That eliminates **(B)**, leaving **(C)** as the correct answer.

For the record: If Lu and Timmons were together, Lu has to be preceded by Jackson and Katz (Rule 1), and Timmons has to be followed by Vega and Wilson (Rule 2). To accomplish that, the order would have to be Jackson first, Katz second, Lu and Timmons third, Vega fourth, and Wilson fifth. However, that puts somebody in every week, leaving no week open for Odede and Zheng to be together.

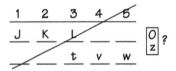

That violates Rule 5, making **(C)** impossible, and thus the correct answer.

23. (D) "If" / Must Be True

For this question, the exhibition with Vega will occur before Katz's exhibition. By Rule 1, Katz's exhibition must precede Lu's, and by Rule 2, the exhibition with Timmons must precede the exhibition with Vega. That arranges four of the five exhibitions. The remaining exhibition must be the one with Odede and Zheng (Rule 5).

$$t \cdots v \begin{smallmatrix} \\ \nearrow \end{smallmatrix} \underline{\quad K \quad} \cdots \underline{\quad L \quad}$$

$$\boxed{\begin{matrix} O \\ z \end{matrix}}?$$

That leaves Jackson and Norales, in either order, for the exhibitions with Timmons and Vega. That leaves Wilson and Yoder, in either order, for Katz's and Lu's exhibition.

$$\boxed{\begin{matrix} J/N \\ t \end{matrix}} \cdots \boxed{\begin{matrix} N/J \\ v \end{matrix}} \cdots \boxed{\begin{matrix} K \\ w/y \end{matrix}} \cdots \boxed{\begin{matrix} L \\ y/w \end{matrix}}$$

$$\boxed{\begin{matrix} O \\ z \end{matrix}}?$$

Based on that, only **(D)** must be true, as the Norales exhibition will feature Timmons or Vega, both of whom perform before Yoder in this situation. The remaining answers all could be true, but need not be.

Glossary

Logical Reasoning

Logical Reasoning Question Types

Argument-Based Questions

Main Point Question

A question that asks for an argument's conclusion or an author's main point. Typical question stems:

> Which one of the following most accurately expresses the conclusion of the argument as a whole?

> Which one of the following sentences best expresses the main point of the scientist's argument?

Role of a Statement Question

A question that asks how a specific sentence, statement, or idea functions within an argument. Typical question stems:

> Which one of the following most accurately describes the role played in the argument by the statement that automation within the steel industry allowed steel mills to produce more steel with fewer workers?

> The claim that governmental transparency is a nation's primary defense against public-sector corruption figures in the argument in which one of the following ways?

Point at Issue Question

A question that asks you to identify the specific claim, statement, or recommendation about which two speakers/authors disagree (or, rarely, about which they agree). Typical question stems:

> A point at issue between Tom and Jerry is

> The dialogue most strongly supports the claim that Marilyn and Billy disagree with each other about which one of the following?

Method of Argument Question

A question that asks you to describe an author's argumentative strategy. In other words, the correct answer describes *how* the author argues (not necessarily what the author says). Typical question stems:

> Which one of the following most accurately describes the technique of reasoning employed by the argument?

> Julian's argument proceeds by

> In the dialogue, Alexander responds to Abigail in which one of the following ways?

Parallel Reasoning Question

A question that asks you to identify the answer choice containing an argument that has the same logical structure and reaches the same type of conclusion as the argument in the stimulus does. Typical question stems:

> The pattern of reasoning in which one of the following arguments is most parallel to that in the argument above?

> The pattern of reasoning in which one of the following arguments is most similar to the pattern of reasoning in the argument above?

Assumption-Family Questions

Assumption Question

A question that asks you to identify one of the unstated premises in an author's argument. Assumption questions come in two varieties.

Necessary Assumption questions ask you to identify an unstated premise required for an argument's conclusion to follow logically from its evidence. Typical question stems:

> Which one of the following is an assumption on which the argument depends?

> Which one of the following is an assumption that the argument requires in order for its conclusion to be properly drawn?

Sufficient Assumption questions ask you to identify an unstated premise sufficient to establish the argument's conclusion on the basis of its evidence. Typical question stems:

> The conclusion follows logically if which one of the following is assumed?

> Which one of the following, if assumed, enables the conclusion above to be properly inferred?

Strengthen/Weaken Question

A question that asks you to identify a fact that, if true, would make the argument's conclusion more likely (Strengthen) or less likely (Weaken) to follow from its evidence. Typical question stems:

Strengthen

Which one of the following, if true, most strengthens the argument above?

Which one the following, if true, most strongly supports the claim above?

Weaken

Which one of the following, if true, would most weaken the argument above?

Which one of the following, if true, most calls into question the claim above?

Flaw Question

A question that asks you to describe the reasoning error that the author has made in an argument. Typical question stems:

The argument's reasoning is most vulnerable to criticism on the grounds that the argument

Which of the following identifies a reasoning error in the argument?

The reasoning in the correspondent's argument is questionable because the argument

Parallel Flaw Question

A question that asks you to identify the argument that contains the same error(s) in reasoning that the argument in the stimulus contains. Typical question stems:

The pattern of flawed reasoning exhibited by the argument above is most similar to that exhibited in which one of the following?

Which one of the following most closely parallels the questionable reasoning cited above?

Evaluate the Argument Question

A question that asks you to identify an issue or consideration relevant to the validity of an argument. Think of Evaluate questions as "Strengthen or Weaken" questions. The correct answer, if true, will strengthen the argument, and if false, will weaken the argument, or vice versa. Evaluate questions are very rare. Typical question stems:

Which one of the following would be most useful to know in order to evaluate the legitimacy of the professor's argument?

It would be most important to determine which one of the following in evaluating the argument?

Non-Argument Questions

Inference Question

A question that asks you to identify a statement that follows from the statements in the stimulus. It is very important to note the characteristics of the one correct and the four incorrect answers before evaluating the choices in Inference questions. Depending on the wording of the question stem, the correct answer to an Inference question may be the one that

- *must be true* if the statements in the stimulus are true

- is *most strongly supported* by the statements in the stimulus

- *must be false* if the statements in the stimulus are true

Typical question stems:

If all of the statements above are true, then which one of the following must also be true?

Which one of the following can be properly inferred from the information above?

If the statements above are true, then each of the following could be true EXCEPT:

Which one of the following is most strongly supported by the information above?

The statements above, if true, most support which one of the following?

The facts described above provide the strongest evidence against which one of the following?

Paradox Question

A question that asks you to identify a fact that, if true, most helps to explain, resolve, or reconcile an apparent contradiction. Typical question stems:

Which one of the following, if true, most helps to explain how both studies' findings could be accurate?

Which one the following, if true, most helps to resolve the apparent conflict in the spokesperson's statements?

Each one of the following, if true, would contribute to an explanation of the apparent discrepancy in the information above EXCEPT:

Principle Questions

Principle Question

A question that asks you to identify corresponding cases and principles. Some Principle questions provide a principle in the stimulus and call for the answer choice describing a case that corresponds to the principle. Others provide a specific case in the stimulus and call for the answer containing a principle to which that case corresponds.

On the LSAT, Principle questions almost always mirror the skills rewarded by other Logical Reasoning question types. After each of the following Principle question stems, we note the question type it resembles. Typical question stems:

Which one of the following principles, if valid, most helps to justify the reasoning above? (**Strengthen**)

Which one of the following most accurately expresses the principle underlying the reasoning above? (**Assumption**)

The situation described above most closely conforms to which of the following generalizations? (**Inference**)

Which one of the following situations conforms most closely to the principle described above? (**Inference**)

Which one of the following principles, if valid, most helps to reconcile the apparent conflict among the prosecutor's claims? (**Paradox**)

Parallel Principle Question

A question that asks you to identify a specific case that illustrates the same principle that is illustrated by the case described in the stimulus. Typical question stem:

Of the following, which one illustrates a principle that is most similar to the principle illustrated by the passage?

Untangling the Stimulus

Conclusion Types

The conclusions in arguments found in the Logical Reasoning section of the LSAT tend to fall into one of six categories:

1) Value Judgment (an evaluative statement; e.g., Action X is unethical, or Y's recital was poorly sung)

2) "If"/Then (a conditional prediction, recommendation, or assertion; e.g., If X is true, then so is Y, or If you are M, then you should do N)

3) Prediction (X *will* or *will not* happen in the future)

4) Comparison (X is taller/shorter/more common/less common, etc. than Y)

5) Assertion of Fact (X is true or X is false)

6) Recommendation (we *should* or *should not* do X)

One-Sentence Test

A tactic used to identify the author's conclusion in an argument. Consider which sentence in the argument is the one the author would keep if asked to get rid of everything except her main point.

Subsidiary Conclusion

A conclusion following from one piece of evidence and then used by the author to support his overall conclusion or main point. Consider the following argument:

The pharmaceutical company's new experimental treatment did not succeed in clinical trials. As a result, the new treatment will not reach the market this year. Thus, the company will fall short of its revenue forecasts for the year.

Here, the sentence "As a result, the new treatment will not reach the market this year" is a subsidiary conclusion. It follows from the evidence that the new treatment failed in clinical trials, and it provides evidence for the overall conclusion that the company will not meet its revenue projections.

Keyword(s) in Logical Reasoning

A word or phrase that helps you untangle a question's stimulus by indicating the logical structure of the argument or the author's point. Here are three categories of Keywords to which LSAT experts pay special attention in Logical Reasoning:

Conclusion words; e.g., *therefore, thus, so, as a result, it follows that, consequently,* [evidence] *is evidence that* [conclusion]

Evidence words; e.g., *because, since, after all, for,* [evidence] *is evidence that* [conclusion]

Contrast words; e.g., *but, however, while, despite, in spite of, on the other hand* (These are especially useful in Paradox and Inference questions.)

Experts use Keywords even more extensively in Reading Comprehension. Learn the Keywords associated with the Reading Comprehension section, and apply them to Logical Reasoning when they are helpful.

Mismatched Concepts

One of two patterns to which authors' assumptions conform in LSAT arguments. Mismatched Concepts describes the assumption in arguments in which terms or concepts in the conclusion are different *in kind* from those in the evidence. The author assumes that there is a logical relationship between the different terms. For example:

Bobby is a **championship swimmer**. Therefore, he **trains every day**.

Here, the words "trains every day" appear only in the conclusion, and the words "championship swimmer" appear only in the evidence. For the author to reach this conclusion from this evidence, he assumes that championship swimmers train every day.

Another example:

> Susan does **not eat her vegetables**. Thus, she will **not grow big and strong**.

In this argument, not growing big and strong is found only in the conclusion while not eating vegetables is found only in the evidence. For the author to reach this conclusion from this evidence, she must assume that eating one's vegetables is necessary for one to grow big and strong.

See also Overlooked Possibilities.

Overlooked Possibilities

One of two patterns to which authors' assumptions conform in LSAT arguments. Overlooked Possibilities describes the assumption in arguments in which terms or concepts in the conclusion are different *in degree, scale, or level of certainty* from those in the evidence. The author assumes that there is no factor or explanation for the conclusion other than the one(s) offered in the evidence. For example:

> Samson does not have a ticket stub for this movie showing. Thus, Samson must have sneaked into the movie without paying.

The author assumes that there is no other explanation for Samson's lack of a ticket stub. The author overlooks several possibilities: e.g., Samson had a special pass for this showing of the movie; Samson dropped his ticket stub by accident or threw it away after entering the theater; someone else in Samson's party has all of the party members' ticket stubs in her pocket or handbag.

Another example:

> Jonah's marketing plan will save the company money. Therefore, the company should adopt Jonah's plan.

Here, the author makes a recommendation based on one advantage. The author assumes that the advantage is the company's only concern or that there are no disadvantages that could outweigh it, e.g., Jonah's plan might save money on marketing but not generate any new leads or customers; Jonah's plan might damage the company's image or reputation; Jonah's plan might include illegal false advertising. Whenever the author of an LSAT argument concludes with a recommendation or a prediction based on just a single fact in the evidence, that author is always overlooking many other possibilities.

See also Mismatched Concepts.

Causal Argument

An argument in which the author concludes or assumes that one thing causes another. The most common pattern on the LSAT is for the author to conclude that A causes B from evidence that A and B are correlated. For example:

> I notice that whenever the store has a poor sales month, employee tardiness is also higher that month. Therefore, it must be that employee tardiness causes the store to lose sales.

The author assumes that the correlation in the evidence indicates a causal relationship. These arguments are vulnerable to three types of overlooked possibilities:

1) There could be **another causal factor**. In the previous example, maybe the months in question are those in which the manager takes vacation, causing the store to lose sales and permitting employees to arrive late without fear of the boss's reprimands.

2) Causation could be **reversed**. Maybe in months when sales are down, employee morale suffers and tardiness increases as a result.

3) The correlation could be **coincidental**. Maybe the correlation between tardiness and the dip in sales is pure coincidence.

See also Flaw Types: Correlation versus Causation.

Another pattern in causal arguments (less frequent on the LSAT) involves the assumption that a particular causal mechanism is or is not involved in a causal relationship. For example:

> The airport has rerouted takeoffs and landings so that they will not create noise over the Sunnyside neighborhood. Thus, the recent drop in Sunnyside's property values cannot be explained by the neighborhood's proximity to the airport.

Here, the author assumes that the only way that the airport could be the cause of dropping property values is through noise pollution. The author overlooks any other possible mechanism (e.g., frequent traffic jams and congestion) through which proximity to the airport could be the cause of Sunnyside's woes.

Principle

A broad, law-like rule, definition, or generalization that covers a variety of specific cases with defined attributes. To see how principles are treated on the LSAT, consider the following principle:

> It is immoral for a person for his own gain to mislead another person.

That principle would cover a specific case, such as a seller who lies about the quality of construction to get a higher price for his house. It would also correspond to the case of a teenager who, wishing to spend a night out on the town, tells his mom "I'm going over to Randy's house." He knows that his mom believes that he will be staying at Randy's house, when in fact, he and Randy will go out together.

That principle does not, however, cover cases in which someone lies solely for the purpose of making the other person feel better or in which one person inadvertently misleads the other through a mistake of fact.

Be careful not to apply your personal ethics or morals when analyzing the principles articulated on the test.

Flaw Types

Necessary versus Sufficient

This flaw occurs when a speaker or author concludes that one event is necessary for a second event from evidence that the first event is sufficient to bring about the second event, or vice versa. Example:

> If more than 25,000 users attempt to access the new app at the same time, the server will crash. Last night, at 11:15 PM, the server crashed, so it must be the case that more than 25,000 users were attempting to use the new app at that time.

In making this argument, the author assumes that the only thing that will cause the server to crash is the usage level (i.e., high usage is *necessary* for the server to crash). The evidence, however, says that high usage is one thing that will cause the server to crash (i.e., that high usage is *sufficient* to crash the server).

Correlation versus Causation

This flaw occurs when a speaker or author draws a conclusion that one thing causes another from evidence that the two things are correlated. Example:

> Over the past half century, global sugar consumption has tripled. That same time period has seen a surge in the rate of technological advancement worldwide. It follows that the increase in sugar consumption has caused the acceleration in technological advancement.

In any argument with this structure, the author is making three unwarranted assumptions. First, he assumes that there is no alternate cause, i.e., there is nothing else that has contributed to rapid technological advancement. Second, he assumes that the causation is not reversed, i.e., technological advancement has not contributed to the increase in sugar consumption, perhaps by making it easier to grow, refine, or transport sugar. And, third, he assumes that the two phenomena are not merely coincidental, i.e., that it is not just happenstance that global sugar consumption is up at the same time that the pace of technological advancement has accelerated.

Unrepresentative Sample

This flaw occurs when a speaker or author draws a conclusion about a group from evidence in which the sample cannot represent that group because the sample is too small or too selective, or is biased in some way. Example:

> Moviegoers in our town prefer action films and romantic comedies over other film genres. Last Friday, we sent reporters to survey moviegoers at several theaters in town, and nearly 90 percent of those surveyed were going to watch either an action film or a romantic comedy.

The author assumes that the survey was representative of the town's moviegoers, but there are several reasons to question that assumption. First, we don't know how many people were actually surveyed. Even if the number of people surveyed was adequate, we don't know how many other types of movies were playing. Finally, the author doesn't limit her conclusion to moviegoers on Friday nights. If the survey had been conducted at Sunday matinees, maybe most moviegoers would have been heading out to see an animated family film or a historical drama. Who knows?

Scope Shift/Unwarranted Assumption

This flaw occurs when a speaker's or author's evidence has a scope or has terms different enough from the scope or terms in his conclusion that it is doubtful that the evidence can support the conclusion. Example:

> A very small percentage of working adults in this country can correctly define collateralized debt obligation securities. Thus, sad to say, the majority of the nation's working adults cannot make prudent choices about how to invest their savings.

This speaker assumes that prudent investing requires the ability to accurately define a somewhat obscure financial term. But prudence is not the same thing as expertise, and the speaker does not offer any evidence that this knowledge of this particular term is related to wise investing.

Percent versus Number/Rate versus Number

This flaw occurs when a speaker or author draws a conclusion about real quantities from evidence about rates or percentages, or vice versa. Example:

> At the end of last season, Camp SunnyDay laid off half of their senior counselors and a quarter of their junior counselors. Thus, Camp SunnyDay must have more senior counselors than junior counselors.

The problem, of course, is that we don't know how many senior and junior counselors were on staff before the layoffs. If there were a total of 4 senior counselors and 20 junior counselors, then the camp would have laid off only 2 senior counselors while dismissing 5 junior counselors.

Equivocation

This flaw occurs when a speaker or author uses the same word in two different and incompatible ways. Example:

> Our opponent in the race has accused our candidate's staff members of behaving unprofessionally. But that's not fair. Our staff is made up entirely of volunteers, not paid campaign workers.

The speaker interprets the opponent's use of the word *professional* to mean "paid," but the opponent likely meant something more along the lines of "mature, competent, and businesslike."

Ad Hominem

This flaw occurs when a speaker or author concludes that another person's claim or argument is invalid because that other person has a personal flaw or shortcoming. One common pattern is for the speaker or author to claim the other person acts hypocritically or that the other person's claim is made from self-interest. Example:

> Mrs. Smithers testified before the city council, stating that the speed limits on the residential streets near her home are dangerously high. But why should we give her claim any credence? The way she eats and exercises, she's not even looking out for her own health.

The author attempts to undermine Mrs. Smithers's testimony by attacking her character and habits. He doesn't offer any evidence that is relevant to her claim about speed limits.

Part versus Whole

This flaw occurs when a speaker or author concludes that a part or individual has a certain characteristic because the whole or the larger group has that characteristic, or vice versa. Example:

> Patient: I should have no problems taking the three drugs prescribed to me by my doctors. I looked them up, and none of the three is listed as having any major side effects.

Here, the patient is assuming that what is true of each of the drugs individually will be true of them when taken together. The patient's flaw is overlooking possible interactions that could cause problems not present when the drugs are taken separately.

Circular Reasoning

This flaw occurs when a speaker or author tries to prove a conclusion with evidence that is logically equivalent to the conclusion. Example:

> All those who run for office are prevaricators. To see this, just consider politicians: they all prevaricate.

Perhaps the author has tried to disguise the circular reasoning in this argument by exchanging the words "those who run for office" in the conclusion for "politicians" in the evidence, but all this argument amounts to is "Politicians prevaricate; therefore, politicians prevaricate." On the LSAT, circular reasoning is very rarely the correct answer to a Flaw question, although it is regularly described in one of the wrong answers.

Question Strategies

Denial Test

A tactic for identifying the assumption *necessary* to an argument. When you negate an assumption necessary to an argument, the argument will fall apart. Negating an assumption that is not necessary to the argument will not invalidate the argument. Consider the following argument:

> Only high schools that produced a state champion athlete during the school year will be represented at the Governor's awards banquet. Therefore, McMurtry High School will be represented at the Governor's awards banquet.

Which one of the following is an assumption necessary to that argument?

> (1) McMurtry High School produced more state champion athletes than any other high school during the school year.

> (2) McMurtry High School produced at least one state champion athlete during the school year.

If you are at all confused about which of those two statements reflects the *necessary* assumption, negate them both.

> (1) McMurtry High School **did not produce more** state champion athletes than any other high school during the school year.

That does not invalidate the argument. McMurtry could still be represented at the Governor's banquet.

> (2) McMurtry High School **did not produce any** state champion athletes during the school year.

Here, negating the statement causes the argument to fall apart. Statement (2) is an assumption *necessary* to the argument.

Point at Issue "Decision Tree"

A tactic for evaluating the answer choices in Point at Issue questions. The correct answer is the only answer choice to which you can answer "Yes" to all three questions in the following diagram.

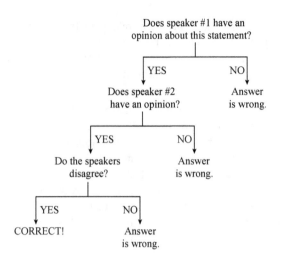

Common Methods of Argument

These methods of argument or argumentative strategies are common on the LSAT:

- Analogy, in which an author draws parallels between two unrelated (but purportedly similar) situations
- Example, in which an author cites a specific case or cases to justify a generalization
- Counterexample, in which an author seeks to discredit an opponent's argument by citing a specific case or cases that appear to invalidate the opponent's generalization
- Appeal to authority, in which an author cites an expert's claim or opinion as support for her conclusion
- Ad hominem attack, in which an author attacks her opponent's personal credibility rather than attacking the substance of her opponent's argument
- Elimination of alternatives, in which an author lists possibilities and discredits or rules out all but one
- Means/requirements, in which the author argues that something is needed to achieve a desired result

Wrong Answer Types in LR

Outside the Scope (Out of Scope; Beyond the Scope)

An answer choice containing a statement that is too broad, too narrow, or beyond the purview of the stimulus, making the statement in the choice irrelevant

180

An answer choice that directly contradicts what the correct answer must say (e.g., a choice that strengthens the argument in a Weaken question)

Extreme

An answer choice containing language too emphatic to be supported by the stimulus; often (although not always) characterized by words such as *all*, *never*, *every*, *only*, or *most*

Distortion

An answer choice that mentions details from the stimulus but mangles or misstates what the author said about those details

Irrelevant Comparison

An answer choice that compares two items or attributes in a way not germane to the author's argument or statements

Half-Right/Half-Wrong

An answer choice that begins correctly, but then contradicts or distorts the passage in its second part; this wrong answer type is more common in Reading Comprehension than it is in Logical Reasoning

Faulty Use of Detail

An answer choice that accurately states something from the stimulus, but does so in a manner that answers the question incorrectly; this wrong answer type is more common in Reading Comprehension than it is in Logical Reasoning

Logic Games

Game Types

Strict Sequencing Game

A game that asks you to arrange entities into numbered positions or into a set schedule (usually hours or days). Strict Sequencing is, by far, the most common game type on the LSAT. In the typical Strict Sequencing game, there is a one-to-one matchup of entities and positions, e.g., seven entities to be placed in seven positions, one per position, or six entities to be placed over six consecutive days, one entity per day.

From time to time, the LSAT will offer Strict Sequencing with more entities than positions (e.g., seven entities to be arranged over five days, with some days to receive more than one entity) or more positions than entities (e.g., six entities to be scheduled over seven days, with at least one day to receive no entities).

Other, less common variations on Strict Sequencing include:

Double Sequencing, in which each entity is placed or scheduled two times (there have been rare occurrences of Triple or Quadruple Sequencing). Alternatively, a Double Sequencing game may involve two different sets of entities each sequenced once.

Circular Sequencing, in which entities are arranged around a table or in a circular arrangement (NOTE: When the positions in a Circular Sequencing game are numbered, the first and last positions are adjacent.)

Vertical Sequencing, in which the positions are numbered from top to bottom or from bottom to top (as in the floors of a building)

Loose Sequencing Game

A game that asks you to arrange or schedule entities in order but provides no numbering or naming of the positions. The rules in Loose Sequencing give only the relative positions (earlier or later, higher or lower) between two entities or among three entities. Loose Sequencing games almost always provide that there will be no ties between entities in the rank, order, or position they take.

Circular Sequencing Game

See Strict Sequencing Game.

Selection Game

A game that asks you to choose or include some entities from the initial list of entities and to reject or exclude others. Some Selection games provide overall limitations on the number of entities to be selected (e.g., "choose exactly four of seven students" or "choose at least two of six entrees") while others provide little or no restriction on the number selected ("choose at least one type of flower" or "select from among seven board members").

Distribution Game

A game that asks you to break up the initial list of entities into two, three, or (very rarely) four groups or teams. In the vast majority of Distribution games, each entity is assigned to one and only one group or team. A relatively common variation on Distribution games will provide a subdivided list of entities (e.g., eight students—four men and four women—will form three study groups) and will then require representatives from those subdivisions on each team (e.g., each study group will have at least one of the men on it).

Matching Game

A game that asks you to match one or more members of one set of entities to specific members of another set of entities,

or that asks you to match attributes or objects to a set of entities. Unlike Distribution games, in which each entity is placed in exactly one group or team, Matching games usually permit you to assign the same attribute or object to more than one entity.

In some cases, there are overall limitations on the number of entities that can be matched (e.g., "In a school's wood shop, there are four workstations—numbered 1 through 4—and each workstation has at least one and at most three of the following tools—band saw, dremmel tool, electric sander, and power drill"). In almost all Matching games, further restrictions on the number of entities that can be matched to a particular person or place will be found in the rules (e.g., Workstation 4 will have more tools than Workstation 2 has).

Hybrid Game

A game that asks you to do two (or rarely, three) of the standard actions (Sequencing, Selection, Distribution, and Matching) to a set of entities.

The most common Hybrid is Sequencing-Matching. A typical Sequencing-Matching Hybrid game might ask you to schedule six speakers at a conference to six one-hour speaking slots (from 9 AM to 2 PM), and then assign each speaker one of two subjects (economic development or trade policy).

Nearly as common as Sequencing-Matching is Distribution-Sequencing. A typical game of this type might ask you to divide six people in a talent competition into either a Dance category or a Singing category, and then rank the competitors in each category.

It is most common to see one Hybrid game in each Logic Games section, although there have been tests with two Hybrid games and tests with none. To determine the type of Hybrid you are faced with, identify the game's action in Step 1 of the Logic Games Method. For example, a game asking you to choose four of six runners, and then assign the four chosen runners to lanes numbered 1 through 4 on a track, would be a Selection-Sequencing Hybrid game.

Mapping Game

A game that provides you with a description of geographical locations and, typically, of the connections among them. Mapping games often ask you to determine the shortest possible routes between two locations or to account for the number of connections required to travel from one location to another. This game type is extremely rare, and as of February 2017, a Mapping game was last seen on PrepTest 40 administered in June 2003.

Process Game

A game that opens with an initial arrangement of entities (e.g., a starting sequence or grouping) and provides rules that describe the processes through which that arrangement can be altered. The questions typically ask you for acceptable arrangements or placements of particular entities after one, two, or three stages in the process. Occasionally, a Process game question might provide information about the arrangement after one, two, or three stages in the process and ask you what must have happened in the earlier stages. This game type is extremely rare, and as of November 2016, a Process game was last seen on PrepTest 16 administered in September 1995. However, there was a Process game on PrepTest 80, administered in December 2016, thus ending a 20-year hiatus.

Game Setups and Deductions

Floater

An entity that is not restricted by any rule or limitation in the game

Blocks of Entities

Two or more entities that are required by rule to be adjacent or separated by a set number of spaces (Sequencing games), to be placed together in the same group (Distribution games), to be matched to the same entity (Matching games), or to be selected or rejected together (Selection games)

Limited Options

Rules or restrictions that force all of a game's acceptable arrangements into two (or occasionally three) patterns

Established Entities

An entity required by rule to be placed in one space or assigned to one particular group throughout the entire game

Number Restrictions

Rules or limitations affecting the number of entities that may be placed into a group or space throughout the game

Duplications

Two or more rules that restrict a common entity. Usually, these rules can be combined to reach additional deductions. For example, if you know that B is placed earlier than A in a sequence and that C is placed earlier than B in that sequence, you can deduce that C is placed earlier than A in the sequence and that there is at least one space (the space occupied by B) between C and A.

Master Sketch

The final sketch derived from the game's setup, rules, and deductions. LSAT experts preserve the Master Sketch for reference as they work through the questions. The Master Sketch does not include any conditions from New-"If" question stems.

Logic Games Question Types

Acceptability Question

A question in which the correct answer is an acceptable arrangement of all the entities relative to the spaces, groups, or selection criteria in the game. Answer these by using the rules to eliminate answer choices that violate the rules.

Partial Acceptability Question

A question in which the correct answer is an acceptable arrangement of some of the entities relative to some of the spaces, groups, or selection criteria in the game, and in which the arrangement of entities not included in the answer choices could be acceptable to the spaces, groups, or selection criteria not explicitly shown in the answer choices. Answer these the same way you would answer Acceptability questions, by using the rules to eliminate answer choices that explicitly or implicitly violate the rules.

Must Be True/False; Could Be True/False Question

A question in which the correct answer must be true, could be true, could be false, or must be false (depending on the question stem), and in which no additional rules or conditions are provided by the question stem

New-"If" Question

A question in which the stem provides an additional rule, condition, or restriction (applicable only to that question), and then asks what must/could be true/false as a result. LSAT experts typically handle New-"If" questions by copying the Master Sketch, adding the new restriction to the copy, and working out any additional deductions available as a result of the new restriction before evaluating the answer choices.

Rule Substitution Question

A question in which the correct answer is a rule that would have an impact identical to one of the game's original rules on the entities in the game

Rule Change Question

A question in which the stem alters one of the original rules in the game, and then asks what must/could be true/false as a result. LSAT experts typically handle Rule Change questions by reconstructing the game's sketch, but now accounting for the changed rule in place of the original. These questions are rare on recent tests.

Rule Suspension Question

A question in which the stem indicates that you should ignore one of the original rules in the game, and then asks what must/could be true/false as a result. LSAT experts typically handle Rule Suspension questions by reconstructing the game's sketch, but now accounting for the absent rule. These questions are very rare.

Complete and Accurate List Question

A question in which the correct answer is a list of any and all entities that could acceptably appear in a particular space or group, or a list of any and all spaces or groups in which a particular entity could appear

Completely Determine Question

A question in which the correct answer is a condition that would result in exactly one acceptable arrangement for all of the entities in the game

Supply the "If" Question

A question in which the correct answer is a condition that would guarantee a particular result stipulated in the question stem

Minimum/Maximum Question

A question in which the correct answer is the number corresponding to the fewest or greatest number of entities that could be selected (Selection), placed into a particular group (Distribution), or matched to a particular entity (Matching). Often, Minimum/Maximum questions begin with New-"If" conditions.

Earliest/Latest Question

A question in which the correct answer is the earliest or latest position in which an entity may acceptably be placed. Often, Earliest/Latest questions begin with New-"If" conditions.

"How Many" Question

A question in which the correct answer is the exact number of entities that may acceptably be placed into a particular group or space. Often, "How Many" questions begin with New-"If" conditions.

Reading Comprehension

Strategic Reading

Roadmap

The test taker's markup of the passage text in Step 1 (Read the Passage Strategically) of the Reading Comprehension Method. To create helpful Roadmaps, LSAT experts circle or underline Keywords in the passage text and jot down brief, helpful notes or paragraph summaries in the margin of their test booklets.

Keyword(s) in Reading Comprehension

Words in the passage text that reveal the passage structure or the author's point of view and thus help test takers anticipate and research the questions that accompany the passage. LSAT experts pay attention to six categories of Keywords in Reading Comprehension:

Emphasis/Opinion—words that signal that the author finds a detail noteworthy or that the author has positive or negative opinion about a detail; any subjective or evaluative language on the author's part (e.g., *especially, crucial, unfortunately, disappointing, I suggest, it seems likely*)

Contrast—words indicating that the author finds two details or ideas incompatible or that the two details illustrate conflicting points (e.g., *but, yet, despite, on the other hand*)

Logic—words that indicate an argument, either the author's or someone else's; these include both Evidence and Conclusion Keywords (e.g., *thus, therefore, because, it follows that*)

Illustration—words indicating an example offered to clarify or support another point (e.g., *for example, this shows, to illustrate*)

Sequence/Chronology—words showing steps in a process or developments over time (e.g., *traditionally, in the past, today, first, second, finally, earlier, subsequent*)

Continuation—words indicating that a subsequent example or detail supports the same point or illustrates the same idea as the previous example (e.g., *moreover, in addition, also, further, along the same lines*)

Margin Notes

The brief notes or paragraph summaries that the test taker jots down next to the passage in the margin of the test booklet

Big Picture Summaries: Topic/Scope/Purpose/Main Idea

A test taker's mental summary of the passage as a whole made during Step 1 (Read the Passage Strategically) of the Reading Comprehension Method. LSAT experts account for four aspects of the passage in their big picture summaries:

Topic—the overall subject of the passage

Scope—the particular aspect of the Topic that the author focuses on

Purpose—the author's reason or motive for writing the passage (express this as a verb; e.g., *to refute*, *to outline*, *to evaluate*, *to critique*)

Main Idea—the author's conclusion or overall takeaway; if the passage does not contain an explicit conclusion or thesis, you can combine the author's Scope and Purpose to get a good sense of the Main Idea.

Passage Types

Kaplan categorizes Reading Comprehension passages in two ways, by subject matter and by passage structure.

Subject matter categories

In the majority of LSAT Reading Comprehension sections, there is one passage from each of the following subject matter categories:

Humanities—topics from art, music, literature, philosophy, etc.

Natural Science—topics from biology, astronomy, paleontology, physics, etc.

Social Science—topics from anthropology, history, sociology, psychology, etc.

Law—topics from constitutional law, international law, legal education, jurisprudence, etc.

Passage structure categories

The majority of LSAT Reading Comprehension passages correspond to one of the following descriptions. The first categories—Theory/Perspective and Event/Phenomenon—have been the most common on recent LSATs.

Theory/Perspective—The passage focuses on a thinker's theory or perspective on some aspect of the Topic; typically (though not always), the author disagrees and critiques the thinker's perspective and/or defends his own perspective.

Event/Phenomenon—The passage focuses on an event, a breakthrough development, or a problem that has recently arisen; when a solution to the problem is proposed, the author most often agrees with the solution (and that represents the passage's Main Idea).

Biography—The passage discusses something about a notable person; the aspect of the person's life emphasized by the author reflects the Scope of the passage.

Debate—The passage outlines two opposing positions (neither of which is the author's) on some aspect of the Topic; the author may side with one of the positions, may remain neutral, or may critique both. (This structure has been relatively rare on recent LSATs.)

Comparative Reading

A pair of passages (labeled Passage A and Passage B) that stand in place of the typical single passage; they have appeared exactly one time in each Reading Comprehension section administered since June 2007. The paired Comparative Reading passages share the same Topic, but may have different Scopes and Purposes. On most LSAT tests, a majority of the questions accompanying Comparative Reading passages require the test taker to compare or contrast ideas or details from both passages.

Question Strategies

Research Clues

A reference in a Reading Comprehension question stem to a word, phrase, or detail in the passage text, or to a particular line number or paragraph in the passage. LSAT experts recognize five kinds of research clues:

Line Reference—An LSAT expert researches around the referenced lines, looking for Keywords that indicate why the referenced details were included or how they were used by the author.

Paragraph Reference—An LSAT expert consults her passage Roadmap to see the paragraph's Scope and Purpose.

Quoted Text (often accompanied by a line reference)—An LSAT expert checks the context of the quoted term or phrase, asking what the author meant by it in the passage.

Proper Nouns—An LSAT expert checks the context of the person, place, or thing in the passage, asking whether the author made a positive, negative, or neutral evaluation of it and why the author included it in the passage.

Content Clues—These are terms, concepts, or ideas from the passage mentioned in the question stem but not as direct quotes and not accompanied by line references. An LSAT expert knows that content clues almost always refer to something that the author emphasized or about which the author expressed an opinion.

Reading Comp Question Types

Global Question

A question that asks for the Main Idea of the passage or for the author's primary Purpose in writing the passage. Typical question stems:

> Which one of the following most accurately expresses the main point of the passage?

> The primary purpose of the passage is to

Detail Question

A question that asks what the passage explicitly states about a detail. Typical question stems:

> According to the passage, some critics have criticized Gilliam's films on the grounds that

> The passage states that one role of a municipality's comptroller in budget decisions by the city council is to

> The author identifies which one of the following as a commonly held but false preconception?

> The passage contains sufficient information to answer which of the following questions?

Occasionally, the test will ask for a correct answer that contains a detail *not* stated in the passage:

> The author attributes each of the following positions to the Federalists EXCEPT:

Inference Question

A question that asks for a statement that follows from or is based on the passage but that is not necessarily stated explicitly in the passage. Some Inference questions contain research clues. The following are typical Inference question stems containing research clues:

> Based on the passage, the author would be most likely to agree with which one of the following statements about unified field theory?

> The passage suggests which one of the following about the behavior of migratory water fowl?

> Given the information in the passage, to which one of the following would radiocarbon dating techniques likely be applicable?

Other Inference questions lack research clues in the question stem. They may be evaluated using the test taker's Big Picture Summaries, or the answer choices may make it clear that the test taker should research a particular part of the passage text. The following are typical Inference question stems containing research clues:

> It can be inferred from the passage that the author would be most likely to agree that

> Which one of the following statements is most strongly supported by the passage?

Other Reading Comprehension question types categorized as Inference questions are Author's Attitude questions and Vocabulary-in-Context questions.

Logic Function Question

A question that asks why the author included a particular detail or reference in the passage or how the author used a particular detail or reference. Typical question stems:

> The author of the passage mentions declining inner-city populations in the paragraph most likely in order to

> The author's discussion of Rimbaud's travels in the Mediterranean (lines 23–28) functions primarily to

> Which one of the following best expresses the function of the third paragraph in the passage?

Logic Reasoning Question

A question that asks the test taker to apply Logical Reasoning skills in relation to a Reading Comprehension passage. Logic Reasoning questions often mirror Strengthen or Parallel Reasoning questions, and occasionally mirror Method of Argument or Principle questions. Typical question stems:

> Which one of the following, if true, would most strengthen the claim made by the author in the last sentence of the passage (lines 51–55)?

> Which one of the following pairs of proposals is most closely analogous to the pair of studies discussed in the passage?

Author's Attitude Question

A question that asks for the author's opinion or point of view on the subject discussed in the passage or on a detail mentioned in the passage. Since the correct answer may follow from the passage without being explicitly stated in it, some Author's Attitude questions are characterized as a subset of Inference questions. Typical question stems:

> The author's attitude toward the use of DNA evidence in the appeals by convicted felons is most accurately described as

> The author's stance regarding monetarist economic theories can most accurately be described as one of

Vocabulary-in-Context Question

A question that asks how the author uses a word or phrase within the context of the passage. The word or phrase in question is always one with multiple meanings. Since the correct answer follows from its use in the passage, Vocabulary-in-Context questions are characterized as a subset of Inference questions. Typical question stems:

> Which one of the following is closest in meaning to the word "citation" as it used in the second paragraph of the passage (line 18)?

> In context, the word "enlightenment" (line 24) refers to

Wrong Answer Types in RC

Outside the Scope (Out of Scope; Beyond the Scope)

An answer choice containing a statement that is too broad, too narrow, or beyond the purview of the passage

180

An answer choice that directly contradicts what the correct answer must say

Extreme

An answer choice containing language too emphatic (e.g., *all*, *never*, *every*, *none*) to be supported by the passage

Distortion

An answer choice that mentions details or ideas from the passage but mangles or misstates what the author said about those details or ideas

Faulty Use of Detail

An answer choice that accurately states something from the passage but in a manner that incorrectly answers the question

Half-Right/Half-Wrong

An answer choice in which one clause follows from the passage while another clause contradicts or deviates from the passage

Contrapositive

The conditional statement logically equivalent to another conditional statement formed by reversing the order of and negating the terms in the original conditional statement. For example, reversing and negating the terms in this statement:

$$\text{If} \quad A \quad \rightarrow \quad B$$

results in its contrapositive:

$$\text{If} \quad \sim B \quad \rightarrow \quad \sim A$$

To form the contrapositive of conditional statements in which either the sufficient clause or the necessary clause has more than one term, you must also change the conjunction *and* to *or*, or vice versa. For example, reversing and negating the terms and changing *and* to *or* in this statement:

$$\text{If} \quad M \quad \rightarrow \quad O \text{ AND } P$$

results in its contrapositive:

$$\text{If} \quad \sim O \text{ OR } \sim P \quad \rightarrow \quad \sim M$$

Formal Logic Terms

Conditional Statement ("If"-Then Statement)

A statement containing a sufficient clause and a necessary clause. Conditional statements can be described in Formal Logic shorthand as:

If [*sufficient clause*] → [*necessary clause*]

In some explanations, the LSAT expert may refer to the sufficient clause as the statement's "trigger" and to the necessary clause as the statement's result.

For more on how to interpret, describe, and use conditional statements on the LSAT, please refer to "A Note About Formal Logic on the LSAT" in this book's introduction.

Printed in the USA
CPSIA information can be obtained
at www.ICGtesting.com
LVHW010205301023
762520LV00022B/390